Elizabeth
Almost by Chance a Woman

DARIO FO was born in 1926 in Lombardy. He began working in the theatre in 1951 as a comic and mime. Together with his wife, Franca Rame, he was highly successful as actor, director and writer of satirical comedies for the conventional theatre. In the Sixties they abandoned it; Fo began to write for a wider audience in factories and workers' clubs and produced work which was not only an important political intervention in Italy but has been internationally acclaimed. In 1970 he and his wife founded the theatrical collective, La Comune, in Milan. His work – and the work of Franca Rame – has been performed in England with great success: *Can't Pay? Won't Pay* (Half Moon Theatre and Criterion Theatre, London, 1981); *Accidental Death of an Anarchist* (Half Moon Theatre and Wyndham's Theatre, London, 1980); *Female Parts* by Franca Rame (National Theatre, London, 1981); *Mistero Buffo* (Riverside Theatre, London, 1983); *Trumpets and Raspberries* (Palace Theatre, Watford; Phoenix Theatre, London, 1984); *Archangels Don't Play Pinball* (Bristol Old Vic, 1986) and *Elizabeth* (Half Moon Theatre, London, 1986).

Also by Dario Fo

Accidental Death of an Anarchist
Archangels Don't Play Pinball
Can't Pay? Won't Pay!
Elizabeth
Female Parts (co-author: Franca Rame)
Trumpets and Raspberries

Series editor: Stuart Hood

DARIO FO

Elizabeth Almost by Chance a Woman

Translated by GILLIAN HANNA
Edited and introduced by STUART HOOD

A Methuen Paperback

A METHUEN MODERN PLAY

This translation first published in 1987 by Methuen London Ltd.,
11 New Fetter Lane, London EC4P 4EE.

Translation copyright © 1987 by Gillian Hanna
Introduction and chronology copyright © 1987 by Stuart Hood

Typeset by Theatretexts, Waterguard House,
1 Branch Road, London E14.

Printed in Great Britain by Richard Clay Ltd,
Bungay, Suffolk

Fo, Dario
    Elizabeth : almost by chance a woman.—
    (A Methuen modern play)
    I. Title II. Hood, Stuart III. Quasi per caso una donna. *English*
    852'.914   PQ4866.02

    ISBN 0-413-15270-7

CAUTION

Contents

INTRODUCTION
The Theatre of Dario Fo and Franca Rame

The son of a railway worker, Dario Fo was born in 1926 near the Lago Maggiore in Northern Italy. He grew up in a village community that included glass-blowers and smugglers, where there was a strong tradition of popular narrative – much of it humorously subversive of authority – fed by travelling story-tellers and puppeteers. Gifted artistically, he studied architecture at Milan at the art-school attached to the Brera Gallery; but the theatre drew him strongly – first as a set-designer and then as a performer. His career began in revue which was the spectacular escapist entertainment of post-war Italy with girls and comics (some very brilliant like Totò, whom Fo greatly admired) and glamorous *chanteuses*. It was a genre favoured by politicians of the ruling Christian Democrat party; girls' legs were preferable to the social preoccupations of contemporary Italian cinema. In revue Fo began to make his mark as an extraordinarily original comic and mime. On radio he built a reputation with his monologues as Poer Nano – the poor simpleton who, in telling Bible stories, for example, gets things wrong, preferring Cain to the insufferable prig, Abel. In 1954 he married Franca Rame, a striking and talented actress, who came from a family of travelling players and had made her first stage appearance when she was eight days old. Together they embarked on a highly successful series of productions.

In the fifties the right-wing clerical Christian Democrat government had imposed a tight censorship on film, theatre and broadcasting. Fo took advantage of a slight relaxation in censorship to mount an 'anti-revue', *Il dito nell'occhio* (One in the Eye). His aim was clear – to attack those myths in Italian life which, as he said, 'Fascism had imposed and Christian Democracy had preserved.' *Il dito nell'occhio* was 'one in the eye' for official versions of history. Presented at the Piccolo Teatro in Milan it was an immense success to which the participation of the great French mime, Jacques Lecoq, from whom Fo learned much, was an important contribution. *Il dito nell'occhio* was the first in a series of pieces which drew on French farce, on the traditional sketches of the Rame family, and on the traditions of the circus. This mixture of spectacle, mime and social comment was highly successful but made the authorities nervous; the police were frequently present at performances, following the scripts with pocket torches to ensure that there were no departures from the officially approved text. Fo grew in stature and virtuosity as actor and comic, exploiting his extraordinary range of gesture, movement and facial expression, his variety of voices and accents, and his skill as a story-teller. It was the misfortune of Italian cinema that it was unable to exploit his talents. There were difficulties in finding suitable scripts and, on set, his vitality and spontaneity were denied the space and freedom that the theatre provided. But what Fo did take away from film was an understanding of how montage gave pace to narrative.

In 1959 the Dario Fo–Franca Rame company was invited to open a season at the Odeon Theatre in Milan. The piece they chose was *Gli arcangeli non giocano a flipper* (Archangels Don't Play Pinball), written, directed and designed by Fo. It was unusual in that it dealt critically with certain ludicrous aspects of Italian society. The middle-class audience were astonished by its rhythms and technique and delighted by Fo in the leading role – that of a wise simpleton, who looks back to Poer Nano and forward to a series of similar clowns in later work. Fo and Rame were now securely established both as actors and as personalities in the public eye. Their success in conventional theatre was confirmed by a series of pieces which exploited a mixture of comedy, music and farcical plots in which Fo would, for instance, double as an absent-minded priest and a bandit. The social references were there – Fo and Rame were now both close to the Communist Party and acutely aware of the political tensions in society – and the public readily picked them up. In a period which saw widespread industrial unrest culminating in the general strike of 1960 their material caused the authorities in Milan to threaten to ban performances.

Italian television had been for many years a fief of the Christian Democrats. Programme control was strict: a young woman given to wearing tight sweaters who looked like winning a popular quiz show had to be eliminated on moral grounds. But when in 1962 the centre-left of the Christian Democrats became dominant there was some relaxation of censorship. It was in these circumstances that the Fo–Rame team was invited to appear on the most popular TV show, *Canzonissima*, which, as its name suggests, featured heart-throb singers along with variety acts. Into this show the Fo's proceeded to inject their own brand of subversive humour – such as a sketch in which a worker whose aunt has fallen into a mincing-machine, which cannot be stopped for that would interrupt production, piously takes her home as tinned meat. The reaction of the political authorities and of the right-wing press was to call for censorship, duly imposed by the obedient functionaries of Italian television – all of them political appointees. There was a tussle of wills at the end of which the Fo's walked out of the show. The scandal was immense. There were parliamentary questions; threats of law-suits on both sides. Fo had public opinion solidly behind him. He had, he said, tried to look behind the facade of the 'economic miracle', to question the view that 'we were all one big family now' and to show how exploitation had increased and scandals flourished. By subverting *Canzonissima* from within he had established himself with a huge popular audience.

During this period Fo had become interested in material set in or drawn from the Middle Ages. He had begun 'to look at the present with the instruments of history and culture in order to judge it better'. He invited the public to use these instruments by writing an ambitious piece, *Isabella, tre caravelle e un cacciaballe* (Isabella, Three Caravels and a Wild-Goose Chaser), in which Columbus – that schoolbook hero – is portrayed as the upwards striving intellectual who loses out in the game of high politics. It was a period when Brecht's *Galileo* was playing with great success in Milan and the theatre was a subject of intense debate in the intellectual and political ferment leading up to the unrest of 1968. For Fo the most important result was probably his collaboration with a group of left-wing musicians who had become interested in the political potential of popular songs. Their work appealed to him because he was himself 'interested above all in a past attached to the roots of the people... and the concept of "the new in the traditional".' They put together a show, built round popular and radical songs, to which Fo contributed his theories on the importance of gesture and the rhythms in the performance of folksong; it marked an important step in his development.

In 1967 he put on his last production for the bourgeois theatre, *La signora non è da buttare* (The Lady's Not For Discarding), in which a circus was made the vehicle for an attack on the United States and capitalist society in general. It again attracted the attention of the authorities. Fo was called to police headquarters in Milan and threatened with arrest for 'offensive lines', not included in the approved version, attacking a head of state – Lyndon Johnson. By now it was becoming 'more and more difficult to act in a theatre where everything down to the subdivision of the seating... mirrored the class divisions. The choice for an intellectual', Fo concluded, 'was to leave his gilded ghetto and put himself at the disposal of the movement.'

The company with which the Fo's confronted this task was the cooperative Nuova Scena – an attempt to dispense with the traditional roles in a stage company and to make decision-making collective. It was, Fo said in retrospect, a utopian project in which individual talents and capabilities were sacrificed to egalitarian principles. But whatever the internal difficulties there was no doubt as to the success the company enjoyed with a new public which it sought out in the working-class estates, in cooperatives and trade union halls, in factories and workers' clubs. It was a public which knew nothing of the theatre but which found the political attitudes the company presented close to its experience of life. Each performance was followed by a discussion.

Nuova Scena did not last long – it was torn apart by political arguments, by arguments over the relationship of art to society and politics, and by questions of organisation. There were also difficulties with the Communist Party, which often controlled the premises used and whose officials began to react negatively to satirical attacks on their bureaucracy, the inflexibility of the Party line, the intolerance of real discussion. Before the split came, the company had put on a *Grande pantomima con bandiere e pupazzi medi e piccoli* (Grand Pantomime with Flags and Little and Medium Puppets), in which Fo used a huge puppet, drawn from the Sicilian tradition, to represent the state and its continual fight with the 'dragon' of the working class. But the most important production was Fo's one-man show *Mistero Buffo*, which was to become one of his enduring triumphs in Italy and abroad. In it he drew on the counter-culture of the Middle Ages, on apocryphal gospel stories, on legend and tales, presenting episodes in which he played all the roles and used a language in part invented, in part archaic, in part drawn from the dialects of Northern Italy. It has been described as 'an imaginary Esperanto of the poor and disinherited'. In performing the scenes of which *Mistero Buffo* is composed – such as the resurrection of Lazarus, the marriage at Cana, Pope Boniface's encounter with Jesus on the Via Dolorosa and others – Fo drew on two main traditions: that of the *giullare* (inadequately translated into English as 'jester'), the travelling comic, singer, mime, who in the Middle Ages was the carrier of a subversive culture; and that of the great clowns of the Commedia dell'Arte with their use of masks, of dialect and of *grammelot*, that extraordinary onomatopoeic rendering of a language – French, say – invented by the 15th-century comedians in which there are accurate sounds and intonations but few real words, all adding up (with the aid of highly expressive mime) to intelligible discourse.

When Nuova Scena split in 1970 it came hard on the heels of mounting polemics in the Communist press. Looking back, Franca Rame has admitted that she and Dario Fo were perhaps sectarian and sometimes mistaken but that they had had to break with the Communist cultural organisations if they wished to progress. The result was La Comune, a theatre company with its headquarters in Milan. The Fo's were now politically linked to the new Left, which found the Communist Party too authoritarian, too locked in the mythology of the Resistance, too inflexible and increasingly conservative. In *Morte accidentale di un'anarchico* (Accidental Death of an Anarchist) Fo produced a piece in which his skill at writing farce and his gifts as a clown were put brilliantly at the service of his politics, playing on the tension between the real death of a prisoner and the farcical inventions advanced by the authorities to explain it. It is estimated that in four years the piece was seen by a million people, many of whom took part in fierce debates after the performance. Fo had succeeded in his aim of making of the theatre 'a great machine which makes people laugh at dramatic things... In the laughter there remains a sediment of anger.' So no easy catharsis. There followed a period in which Fo was deeply engaged politically – both through his writings and through his involvement with Franca Rame, who was the main mover of the project – in Red Aid, which collected funds and comforts for Italian political prisoners detained in harsh conditions. His writing dealt with the Palestinian struggle, with Chile, with the methods of the Italian police. In the spring of 1973 Franca Rame was kidnapped from her home in Milan by a Fascist gang, gravely assaulted and left bleeding in the street. Fo himself later that year was arrested and held in prison in Sardinia for refusing to allow police to be present at rehearsals. Demonstrations and protests ensured his release. Dario Fo had, as his lawyer said, for years no longer been only an actor but a political figure whom the state powers would use any weapon to silence.

His political flair was evident in the farce *Non si paga, non si paga* (Can't Pay? Won't Pay!) dating from 1974, which deals with the question of civil disobedience. Significantly, the main upholder of law and order is a Communist shop steward, who disapproves of his wife's gesture of rebellion against the rising cost of living – a raid on a supermarket. It was a piece tried out on and altered at the suggestion of popular audiences – a practice Fo has often used. It was the same spirit that inspired his *Storia di una tigre* (Story of a Tiger), an allegorical monologue dating from 1980 – after a trip to China, and based on a Chinese folktale – the moral of which is that, if you have 'tiger' in you, you must never delegate responsibility to others, never expect others to solve your own problems, and above all avoid that unthinking party loyalty which is the enemy of reason and of revolution. In 1981, following on the kidnapping of Aldo Moro came *Clacson, trombette e pernacchi* (Trumpets and Raspberries). In it Fo doubled as Agnelli, the boss of FIAT, and a FIAT shop steward, whose identities become farcically confused. The play mocks the police and their readiness to see terrorists everywhere and the political cynicism which led to Moro's being abandoned to his fate by his fellow-politicians.

It was the last of Fo's major political works to date. Looking for new fields at a time when the great political upsurge has died away and the consumerist state has apparently triumphed, Fo has turned in recent years to a play on Elizabeth and Essex, with a splendid transvestite part for himself which allows him to use the dialect of *Mistero Buffo*, and a Harlequinade – a slight but charming piece that returns to the techniques of the Commedia dell'Arte.

Meanwhile Franca Rame, who has progressively established herself as a political figure and a powerful feminist, has produced a number of one-woman plays, partly in collaboration with her husband – monologues which are a direct political intervention in a society where the role of women is notably restricted by the Church, the state and male traditions. Like all their work the one-woman plays such as *Il risveglio* (Waking Up) or *Una donna sola* (A Woman Alone) depend on the tension between the unbearable nature of the situation in which the female protagonist finds herself and the grotesque behaviour of people around her – in particular the men. It is a theme which is treated with anger and disgust in

Lo stupro (The Rape), tragically in her version of *Medea* and comically in *Coppia aperta* (Open Couple) in which the hypocrisies of 'sexual liberation' are dissected.

Dario Fo and Franca Rame have a world-wide reputation. The Scandinavian countries were among the first to welcome them as performers and to produce their work. The whole of Western Europe has by now acknowledged their importance and virtuosity. Ironically the Berliner Ensemble, the theatre founded by Brecht to whom Fo owes so much, found Fo's rock version of *The Beggar's Opera* too difficult to take in spite of Brecht's advice to treat famous authors with disrespect if you have the least consideration for the ideas they express. It had to be staged in Italy. Foreign travel has not been without its problems: attacks on the theatre where they played in Buenos Aires under military rule and a visa to the United States long refused. The summer of 1986 saw the American administration at last relent, which may be some sort of comment on how they judge the Fo's impact and importance in the present political climate.

* * * * *

Elizabeth: Almost by Chance a Woman – to give the play its full title – was written and first performed in 1984. It is essentially a piece for two virtuoso players. The characters are Queen Elizabeth of England, the Virgin Queen of the history books, and Dame Grosslady, a bawdy dealer in patent medicines. These are roles created originally to fit the talents of Franca Rame as the love-torn queen, whose paranoia reads conspiracies into Shakespeare's plays, and Dario Fo, in a transvestite part, as a licensed jester who has an ability to see through to the truth of things not granted to ordinary people – and not even to queens. Both are demanding parts: the queen's passion, fears and nightmares come to their climax at the end of the play in a monologue which is as taxing as an operatic aria; Dame Grosslady comments on life, on sex, on power and on Shakespeare's *Hamlet* in the extraordinary jargon Fo has created out of North Italian dialects and archaisms as a vehicle for his clowns. In the present English version Gillian Hanna has created a brilliantly effective equivalent out of elements from an interesting variety of sources: pseudo-Elizabethan grammatical structures, Elizabethan slang (drawn from Nashe, the chronicler of the Elizabethan underworld), Italian words and pronunciations, Cockney rhyming slang, spoonerisms, puns, and regional expressions from Scotland, Ireland, Norfolk, Yorkshire and elsewhere, together with words drawn from a dictionary of eighteenth-century slang. When reading or acting Dame Grosslady, a knowledge of Italian pronunciation is essential, but it should NOT be performed with an 'Italian' accent. Different cultures might produce different versions of Grosslady's part – one can imagine one, for example, in the language of the black poet, Linton Kwesi Johnson. This edition therefore includes in an appendix Gillian Hanna's plain-language text of that role.

Audiences and critics have come to expect of Dario Fo politically radical plays. *Elizabeth* is not in an obvious sense political although an Italian audience would quickly pick up political references. One is to the so-called 'repenters' – members of organisations like the Red Brigades who in prison 'repented' and turned into super-grasses. (There are obvious parallels in Northern Ireland.) There is the business of rival secret services, penetrating each other and plotting risings: a clear reference to the tangled web of conspiracies involving various secret state agencies in the Italy of the seventies. Yet another is the way central authorities turn a deaf ear to appeals for help from hostages on the grounds that any dealings with terrorists must be taken as a sign of weakness. This relates to the fate of the kidnapped Christian Democrat politician, Aldo Moro, whose letters from captivity in the hands of the Red Brigades were dismissed as embarrassing evidence of mental collapse and whose death-sentence was scaled by his own colleagues in the name of firm government.

There is behind the plot of Fo's play a certain historical substance in that her lover – but what does that mean? – the Earl of Essex, did conspire against Elizabeth and was duly executed. Shakespeare was a member of Essex's circle; indeed some scholars have seen in Hamlet a reflection of Essex's indecisive character. But as Fo himself disarmingly says, historical accuracy is not his aim. He is more interested in the terrible nature of power wielded by persons who can send others to their deaths. Allied to that is the theme which gives the play its driving force: how in a world where she is a rare exception among men, a woman of strength and beauty, endowed with a passionate nature, faces age, fears over the loss of sexual power, and fears of death.

STUART HOOD
January 1987

Author's Note

'Be Careful, This is a Forgery.' This legend should be printed on the frontispiece of the text of *Almost by Chance a Woman: Elizabeth*. Certain sentences attributed to Shakespeare are forgeries; many allusions to historical facts are forgeries; certain characters who appear on stage are downright forgeries, to say nothing of those who are referred to from time to time. Yet the body of the text is, I assure you, laden with authenticity.

It is an absurd text with great probability of truthfulness. The first idea was to play a Boccaccianesque practical joke. I was thinking of having it printed by a friend, a printer, a great craftsman-artist, on ancient paper with seventeenth-century lettering, and of entrusting it to a researcher with a great sense of humour who was to publish it with modern lettering, footnotes and introduction, and then entrust it to me and Franca for us to produce. We would have laughed ourselves silly for years over what the critics would have written. But it would have been too hard a joke – too cruel.

Another legend to be affixed to this text is: 'Comedy in the old Italian style' – in particular of the first half of the seventeenth century. The setting – the fixed interior – is classical of the period. The restricted number of characters is a constant of the Italian theatre of that time.*The presence of the pseudo-procuress, pseudo-Celestina is also a classical element of the period. One only needs to think of Della Porta's 'Fiorina' or Ruzzante's 'Anconitano'. But the element that makes the greatest reference to the Italian theatre of the seventeenth century is the character of the absent protagonist. As in Macchiavelli's 'Clizia', here, the Earl of Essex never appears on stage. He is announced, he is expected, he is sighed for, but he never appears.

I will refrain from telling you that the drama is that of a woman's conflict in her relationship to power – you can work that out for yourselves.

There is only one particular I would like to point out to you: the final monologue† is constructed like a mosaic, borrowing various phrases from Shakespeare's most famous plays from Henry IV to Henry V, from Measure for Measure to Julius Caesar... so you can amuse yourselves by recognising them... I have put in some phrases of my own to link them up... just for the pleasure of masking the sources and to fabricate a genuine forgery.

DARIO FO
London, August 1986

* Celestina is the bawd in a famous Spanish novel in dramatic form – *The Tragi-comedy of Calisto and Melibea* (1499) by Fernando de Rojas.
† The final monologue in Gillian Hanna's translation is also a Shakespearian mosaic although the quotations are not necessarily the same as in the original.

Note: Where this translation departs from the Italian is indicated by a line in the margin. A literal translation is given in the appendix at the end of the play.

This translation of Elizabeth was first staged at the Half Moon Theatre, London on November 3, 1986. The cast was as follows:

YOUNG MAN	Nick Bartlett
ASSASSIN	David Bradford
MARTHA	Angela Curran
ELIZABETH	Gillian Hanna
DAME GROSSLADY	Bob Mason
EGERTON	Jonathan Oliver

Directed by Michael Batz and Chris Bond
Designed by Andrea Montag.

Act One
Scene One

The scene is set in the style of the Italian Renaissance, on two levels, with an open gallery at the back of the upper level, a door in the right-hand corner, and a staircase running down beside the wall. In each arch of the gallery is a window. On the lower level, a door in the right wall, and another in the left.

In the centre, a bed, a facsimile of the famous nuptial bed of Federigo Da Montefeltro. The space on the left is hidden by a double screen on two parallel tapestries, one behind the other, facing the audience. The tapestries can be drawn back. Behind the second one is hidden a lifesize wooden horse on wheels. On the left wall, a large fireplace and a mirror. Near the fireplace, close to the proscenium arch, is a lectern with an inkstand, pen, papers and a sword.

In the centre, clearly visible, a tailor's dummy on which there is a woman's ceremonial dress – black with a white ruff.

A Version of the 'Candy' song

('Candia')

When thou dost cease to love me more,
I'll set my ship for Candy's shore,
And on my billowing sail will blow
Thine eyes in glowing colours, so
When water drown the bridge, oh then I'll see
Thee weep those tears thou ne'er didst weep for me.

And on the prow, there will I place
A carvèd figure-head; thy face,
Thy breasts, thy belly, all will drown
Each time my flying ship dips down

Beneath the water; by the sea held fast,
Those arms that twined round me thou never hast.

And when I come to Candy's sun,
They'll ask me why my sail doth run
So swift, all painted with those eyes;
And I'll reply: 'Let me be wise;
I keep my woman, dear, so close above
In hopes perchance I can forget her love.'

The play begins with the song 'Candia'. *The light is dark, almost blackout. The tapestries are drawn to prevent the audience seeing the horse. As the song finishes,* ELIZABETH *enters, papers in hand. Because of the darkness she bumps into the dummy.*

ELIZABETH: Well, where's everyone got to… ? Martha! Let's get going… (*She finds herself entwined with the dummy*) …What's this? …Martha, why must you keep everything shut up… ? (*She draws the downstage tapestry. A ray of light falls on the dummy.* ELIZABETH *screams*) …AAAHH!! Damned Stuart! (*She takes the sword from the desk*) …Get away! You don't frighten me…

She turns to a curtain on the right which is moving, and lunges at it with her sword.

ELIZABETH: And neither do you! I've seen you… you bastard! I'll run you through!

She sinks the blade into the tapestry.

MARTHA: (*From behind the tapestry – terrified*) Help! Stop it! Elizabeth!

ELIZABETH: Who is it? Come out of there or I'll kill you!

MARTHA: (*Entering*) It's me, Martha… What on earth's got into you?

ELIZABETH: Martha? What were you up to behind there? Were you spying on me?

MARTHA: Don't talk nonsense. I heard you screaming… What's the matter?

Using a pole, she draws back the hanging in front of the window – the ray of light which crosses the room falls full on the dummy. Elizabeth screams again, and hurls the papers at it.

ELIZABETH: There, there... It's Mary! ...The Stuart woman!

MARTHA: No dear, no. It's only her dress... Calm down.

ELIZABETH: Who brought it in here and put it on that headless dummy?

MARTHA: You ordered it to be fetched out of her wardrobe... You wanted to give it to someone... I don't know who.

She removes the dress from the dummy and takes it off stage.

ELIZABETH: That's not true. As a matter of fact, I asked for it to be got out... so it could be aired, that's all.

MARTHA: Well, there's obviously been a little misunderstanding.

ELIZABETH: Misunderstanding, my arse! Someone's done it on purpose. Stuck it there on the dummy... without a head... to give me a heart attack! Whose charming idea was this? I want him brought here immediately!

MARTHA: Very well... I'll get on to it straight away... I'll summon all the servants... and we'll have a nice inquest. Then everyone will know that the queen is still haunted by the ghost of Mary of Scotland.

ELIZABETH: I am not haunted... I couldn't give a monkey's fart about that slag Mary of Scotland!

MARTHA: Well then, prove it. Calm down and get back into bed.

She goes to open the doors of the bed.

ELIZABETH: Leave them alone. Don't open the doors of my bed!

MARTHA: (*Lowering her voice*) Why not? Got a visitor in there? Bloody hell, you must have woken him up with all the squealing you've been doing!

ELIZABETH: There's no one to wake up. I didn't have anyone in my bed last night.

MARTHA: Why don't I open it up then?

ELIZABETH: No, I said. I didn't have anyone in last night, but the one I had three nights ago might still be there.

MARTHA: O for heaven's sake! All right… You're being impossible this morning. What's got into you? Look what you've done… you've scattered these papers all over the place with your flapping about.

She picks up a few.

ELIZABETH: O yes. Give me those.

MARTHA: What is all this stuff?

ELIZABETH: Why don't you tell me? Who is this bastard? Does he write these slanders all on his own? Or maybe he's just an imbecile? I haven't slept a wink all night, trying to work it out.

MARTHA: Elizabeth, will you please calm down… It's me who can't work anything out… Who are you talking about?

ELIZABETH: Shakespeare. Who is this Shakespeare?

MARTHA: Shakespeare? Not again! What's he done to you this time?

ELIZABETH: I told you to find all this out at least a month ago. I want to read every page he's ever written… I want to know how much of this crap he's managed to get on the stage… who prints it…

MARTHA: (*Pointing to the papers she's just finished picking up*) Considering all the really appalling problems you've got to contend with, I can't see why you're working yourself into a lather over these silly melodramas. Now really, this is becoming an obsession.

ELIZABETH: Of course: Elizabeth is mad. She's off her head! Sit down here and look at this… (*She shows her the papers*) …tell me that here in this Henry IV, and again here, in this Richard III, he isn't talking about me… my life… my system of government…

MARTHA: But he didn't make any of this up: it's history.

ELIZABETH: Yes, well, maybe I can't get pissed off with history for copying my life, but I can get pissed off with this creeping bastard for putting it up on the stage as plain as a pike-staff!

MARTHA: So now you're the queen of fairyland too.

ELIZABETH: Fairyland? (*Shows her more papers*) All right then, look at Hamlet: are you trying to tell me it's not an exact portrait of me? Tell me it's not!

MARTHA: Hamlet a portrait of you?

ELIZABETH: Yes. Don't stand there with your mouth hanging open. Have you read it?

MARTHA: No… I barely know the plot.

ELIZABETH: Then read it. Very carefully. You'll find my expressions in it… my cries of despair… my curses… things I've shouted here, in this room. How did this Shakespeare know all this? Who's the spy in here? Martha!

MARTHA: Listen, if you're looking at me… just say the word… I'll start packing now.

ELIZABETH: O stop it… you haven't got the imagination to be an informer. Stop it!

MARTHA: Thank you very much. Anyway, if you could possibly learn to shout a little more quietly, you might avoid being overneard by the guards in the corridor and secretaries passing by, not to mention stray villains hanging about outside your door, or even any young layabout who happened to be tucked up in your bed…

Points to the closed doors of the bed.

ELIZABETH: So now you're going to gang up with all the muckrakers too, are you?

MARTHA: Well I'm good at muckraking, I'm the one who makes your bed every morning.

ELIZABETH: I suppose that's true.

MARTHA: Anyway, if you really want to find out what's at the back of these plays, why don't you ask your Chief of Police... ?

ELIZABETH: Who? Egerton? Where is he?

MARTHA: He's out in the corridor where he's been since daybreak. If you want, I'll let him in.

ELIZABETH: Let him in? So he can find out what a ghoul I am first thing in the morning? If that damn spy-master catches the merest glimpse of me, tomorrow the whole of London will have a detailed description of what a horror I am in my natural state.

MARTHA: Very well. As you wish. He'll have to wait till you've been renovated. (*Ironically*) I'll tell him to come back in four hours. This afternoon.

ELIZABETH: (*Dry*) Ho ho ho. Very witty! All right, let him in. But put something in front of me so he can't see me... O never mind, I'll do it myself... I'll shift my horse... that'll do it...

She draws back the second tapestry to reveal the horse which she pushes to the centre.

MARTHA: (*At the door to the top of the stairs*) Please, Egerton. Do come in. Her Majesty is waiting for you.

EGERTON *enters. He is holding a folder under his arm.*

EGERTON: Thank you. Good morning, Your Highness...

Looks around.

ELIZABETH: Good morning, Egerton.

EGERTON: (*To Martha*) Where is she?

ELIZABETH: I am here, behind... behind the horse. I'm warning you, Egerton, if you so much as poke your nose round the neck of this animal to try and get a glimpse of me... (*She gets a pistol out of her bodice*) ...I'll put a bullet right between your eyes, you little sneak. (*She points the* *pistol round the neck of the horse at* EGERTON) What news have you got for me?

EGERTON: Your Majesty, I am mortified. I can see that you are angry with me.

ELIZABETH: 'Angry'... that's such a little word, Egerton. I am beside myself with fury. In the first place because you have as yet given me no information about the thugs who fired on me from the riverbank when I was out in my barge: I don't know if they were Irishmen, Puritans, Papists, or hunters who mistook me for a golden cockerel...

MARTHA *goes out, and returns with a large basin and towels. She washes* ELIZABETH'*s feet.*

ELIZABETH: Secondly: because I am still trying to find out what criteria you use when you examine texts submitted to you to be licensed for performance. And you are supposed to be the head of my Intelligence Service? Imbecile service, you're the head of.

EGERTON: Your Majesty, I am ready to submit myself to any insult. However, allow me to reassure you that the desperado in question has been apprehended and has talked.

ELIZABETH: Of his own free will?

EGERTON: Yes. Once we applied a burning brand to his feet...

ELIZABETH: For the love of God, Egerton, still using these criminal devices... it's inhuman.

EGERTON: But Your Majesty... It's as old as the world itself. If the police force wants to get confessions, it is obliged...

ELIZABETH: (*Interrupting him*) Obliged my arse! How can I make you understand? We're not living in my father Henry VIII's time any more. Then, they quite simply regarded torture as out-and-out amusement for the interrogators. No. Nowadays we live in a free, humanitarian state, and it's my duty to be shocked, to reproach you... to drag you in front of a court if I catch you in the act. Your duty is to continue the torture nonetheless. But you're not supposed to come running to tell me about it. For God's sake, Egerton, you've ruined my day.

EGERTON: You are right. Forgive me. The one thing we know for certain is that none of this has anything to do with the Earl of Essex.

ELIZABETH: Ah. (*With emotion*) Robert, Robert. (*To* EGERTON) You're just saying that to humour me. You know I love him to distraction.

EGERTON: No, Your Majesty, it is the truth. We have a fanatic on our hands. A single lunatic.

ELIZABETH: How can he be single if there were two of them?

EGERTON: Yes. Two single lunatics.

ELIZABETH: I see. In a while you'll discover there were three of them... or four... The National Association of Single Lunatics... You are pathetic and repetitious... Whenever the instigators of any piece of crap look like being discovered, you're terrified in case the names turn out to be well-known ones, so you come up with this ridiculous refrain about the single lunatic!

EGERTON: Perhaps you are right, Your Majesty... we are repetititous... But I can assure you that in this instance, the Earl of Essex has nothing to do with it.

ELIZABETH: In this instance? Then does he have anything to do with any other instance? Come on. Speak.

EGERTON: I am very much afraid that he may be getting caught up in an enterprise that is truly insane.

ELIZABETH: Is that so? And you, Egerton, along with the rest of my councillors, are gloating.

EGERTON: Your Majesty... I beg you... we... the fact is that the Earl is allowing himself to become the unwitting tool of militant extremists. They are trying to persuade him to organise a serious popular revolt, backed by a supporting invasion.

ELIZABETH: Supporting invasion by whom? From where?

EGERTON: They are trying to involve your cousin, the King of Scotland.

ELIZABETH: James?

EGERTON: Yes. They want him to send his troops to support them when the revolt breaks out...

ELIZABETH: They couldn't be such fuckwits... bloody...

MARTHA: Now, now, Elizabeth. Remember you're a lady as well as a Queen.

ELIZABETH: And I'm the Pope of my own religion as well! And if you don't shut your mouth I'll excommunicate you! Get out.

MARTHA goes out, taking the basin and towels.

ELIZABETH: It's not true, Egerton... All lies! Proof, I want the proof!

MARTHA re-enters.

EGERTON: And here it is, Your Majesty.

He gets some sheets of paper out of a folder and holds them out to the QUEEN without looking at them. She stays hidden behind the horse.

EGERTON: It is a letter written in the hand of the Earl of Essex.

He makes a slight movement in her direction.

ELIZABETH: (*She stops him with the pistol*) Stop there, or I shoot!

She reads the letter intently.

ELIZABETH: 'Now is the time to act! Swiftly! A more propitious moment can hardly come again. The whole country is exasperated, convinced that the Queen is now totally at the mercy of her councillors, who, with their disgraceful political actions, are leading England to her destruction.' (*She laughs*) Martha, come here and look at this! (*Shows the letter to MARTHA*) It's a forgery. It's a ridiculously clumsy imitation of Robert of Essex's handwriting. It's a forgery. Intelligence Service!

EGERTON: Is it possible? But the courier was one of our own men... He assured us...

ELIZABETH: Be quiet! It's a forgery, I said! Or perhaps, Egerton, you doubt my word against that of some infiltrator who is no doubt playing James's game?

EGERTON: O heavens! I don't know what to say... well, it's simple enough to check up on...

ELIZABETH: There you are! Well done! Check up on it! Question him, yes. Arrest him, this trusty collaborator of yours, and apply the Rule of Repentance.

EGERTON: The Rule of Repentance?

ELIZABETH: Of course. My brother Edward thought it up. First you frighten the hell out of the prisoner by showing him the gallows... then suddenly you promise him his freedom, and money if he will grass... He'll begin denouncing people like a supergrass before you've had time to blink... you'll have to plead with him to stop before the prisons start bursting at the seams!

EGERTON: Of course, Your Majesty... I will let you know as soon as possible.

ELIZABETH: Keep me informed, Egerton.

EGERTON: Straight away. (*He bids her farewell*) Your Majesty... Your devoted...

He bows to MARTHA. *He exits, leaving his folder on a chair.*

ELIZABETH: Your devoted arsehole!

She pushes the horse back to its original position.

MARTHA: Pardon me, Elizabeth, I happened to catch a glimpse of those letters... I was struck by your vehemence... there's no doubt?

ELIZABETH: No, no doubt at all. I am absolutely certain. That letter was written by Robert of Essex himself.

MARTHA: (*Gobsmacked*) Ah! Now what?

ELIZABETH: Be quiet. Shut up. Do you expect me to condemn him to death? Am I supposed to have his head chopped off? What use is a man with no head to me? I love him, the wretch. And anyway, you said yourself that perhaps it was my own fault if Robert's gone mad like this.

MARTHA: That's right, stand up for him! Protect him! Your Knave of Hearts... just watch out he doesn't pick up too many trump cards... or the Joker... that would really be a laugh!

She goes out and comes straight back, carrying a tray with cups and teapot. She serves the QUEEN.

ELIZABETH: The Joker? You've understood nothing. Robert Devereux already had the Joker. I was the Joker! But the idiot didn't know how to play me... he threw me away like the two of spades! What's more, he's organising coups against me, surrounding himself with a bunch of halfwits, each more halfwitted than Robert himself. And Egerton and Cecil and Bacon have completely filled the group with infiltrators, spies and agents provocateurs... And the poor little sod hasn't even noticed! What the hell does he think he's up to? Bloody little bollocks! When I think that last night he started a coup...

MARTHA: Who, Essex and his men?

ELIZABETH: Yes. About fifty of them attacked the Armoury in the Old Palace and they filched a whole pile of arms. And it seems as though Egerton knew all about it. But said nothing. Fortunately, I have a second even more secret police force of my own, and I've completely infiltrated his secret police force with my secret secret police force, and they keep me informed about everything, secretly. (*Ironic*) This system is known as 'parliamentary democracy'. So they attacked the Armoury, and whistled out a bunch of weapons. They even nicked two culverins. I'm mad about my culverins. (*Takes up the story again*) I must say, they came up with a rather ingenious trick.

MARTHA: Wonderful!

ELIZABETH: Overjoyed are you? O, look at her... pretends to be so hard-hearted, don't you? But I can see you've got a soft spot for the Knave of Hearts too.

MARTHA: No. Just a minute. I was only admiring the courage and intelligence...

ELIZABETH: Whose intelligence? Robert of Essex? His head is so empty that if an idea ever did pop into it, it would die of loneliness. (*Hands* MARTHA *a cup*) Drink your tea. You're forgetting Egerton's infiltrators. Now they are intelligent. This attack on the Armoury was planned here in the palace... by my men, sat round a desk, with the intention of screwing Robert once and for all.

MARTHA: All right. It's certain that Egerton must have known about Essex's plan to get the arms out of the Palace.

ELIZABETH: Yes, but he left them alone to get on with it. You always let the victim of a sting win the first three rounds so that you can smash them all the harder in the end. Cecil my beloved councillor... Bacon... Knollys... the whole lot of them, including the Privy Council, they all want to teach me a lesson. They can never forgive me for having showered the boy with gifts and leases and appointments. I love him... and I give him presents, I give him presents. When I think of his insolence, that damned pygmy... shouting at me... 'One of these fine days he'll put a saddle on your rump, this Essex of yours! Like a heifer... !' He called me a heifer, do you hear?

MARTHA: Who dared say that? Which pygmy are you talking about?

ELIZABETH: Cecil... my adored councillor. I took no notice of him. I was completely indifferent, as if he'd never even opened his mouth. I just spat in his eye. Bullseye, Martha, it was brilliant. SPLAT! And it wasn't just a lucky shot either... I spent three months practising how to put out a lighted candle at ten paces... and then I booted all their arses out of the door, swearing like a trooper.

MARTHA: They want to get their own back now!

She takes the tray and begins to go.

ELIZABETH: They will bring me his head on a platter like John the Baptist. If I could only talk to him, the idiot!

MARTHA: (*Embarrassed*) I've talked to him.

ELIZABETH: You? When?

MARTHA: Three days ago. I went to look for him. Now I want to make this quite clear. I only did it for your sake. I heard you weeping all night... calling out his name...

ELIZABETH: Why did he agree to see you? Come on, be brave.

MARTHA: (*Even more embarrassed and reluctant*) I told him a little fib.

ELIZABETH: What fib?

MARTHA: Yes, but you mustn't be angry... do you promise?

ELIZABETH: I promise. Queen's word of honour.

MARTHA: I told him you sent me.

ELIZABETH: (*Kicks the tray that MARTHA is holding. The cups smash on the ground*) O, slag... bitch... you stinking...

MARTHA: Now now. You promised. Queen's word of honour.

ELIZABETH: Who gives a fuck... I'll split you in two... I'll murder you...

She snatches up the copper pot and goes to hit her with it.

MARTHA: (*Shouting, trying to block her*) Calm down, Elizabeth. Robert Devereux didn't believe me anyway.

ELIZABETH: (*Complete change of voice. As if nothing had happened*) Martha. What are you shouting about? Say 'He didn't believe me' and leave it at that. There are times when you make me want to smash my copper pot over your head. (*Takes up the story again*) He didn't believe you.

She absent-mindedly picks up the folder that EGERTON left behind.

MARTHA: No! He's still sulking about the last time... he says you humiliated him in front of everyone… am I allowed to know what you called him that was so offensive?

ELIZABETH: Gigolo and rent-boy!

She opens the folder and glances at the contents while she talks to MARTHA.

MARTHA: Rent-boy? Are you out of your mind?

ELIZABETH: But he'd infuriated me. He gave me a shitty little smile and called me 'crooked carcass' and 'withered'… What do you say to that?

MARTHA: It's not very nice…

She picks up the cups that had fallen on the floor.

ELIZABETH: It's not very nice, no. But I had my revenge. I took back the earring I'd given him…

MARTHA: Good for you!

ELIZABETH: Yes. I bit off his earlobe.

MARTHA: That seems a bit excessive to me…

ELIZABETH: Well, I gave it back to him… the earlobe.

She buries her nose in the contents of EGERTON'*s folder.*

MARTHA: Well, the fact is that when I tried to warn him about what I knew… the infiltrators and spies… you're not listening to me…

MARTHA: Yes, yes. I'm listening. Go on…

MARTHA: What are you reading?

ELIZABETH: It's Egerton's file… he forgot it… or maybe he left it behind on purpose. They're copies of letters from various ambassadors to their respective masters…

MARTHA: Heavens! And Egerton, the spy-master, opened the envelopes?

ELIZABETH: Of course. It's all part of the Intelligence Service! He has solvent saliva… one lick… he opens them, copies them and sends them off again. O, look at these. They're all about me. Listen, listen, this is how the

Venetian ambassador honours me. (*She reads*) 'The Queen of England shows off by quoting Latin and Greek, but more than anything else, she loves to laugh in the most gross and vulgar fashion. She tells filthy jokes that would make a brothel-keeper blush. She swears… An Italian clown taught her how to blow the most disgusting raspberries, and these she graciously bestows on those lords who have fallen into disfavour. I have even seen her spit on one of them…' (*She laughs. Very amused*) So he was there too!

MARTHA: International celebrity at last…

ELIZABETH: (*Still reading*) 'She dances like a madwoman, doing incredible jumps. And she sweats so much that when she does pirouettes she soaks the onlookers, like a wet dog that's just got out of the water.'

MARTHA: Well that's true enough. When you're in a state, you do soak everything.

ELIZABETH: Now the Portuguese ambassador thinks I'm really charming… Listen how he describes me: 'A wooden doll. A bloodless puppet decked out in frills and furbelows. A sumptuous gown out of which sprouts a head of glass.' Scumbag! Papist shit! (*To* MARTHA) That's not written down. I said that. Listen. Here's more… 'Elizabeth is terrifying, even when she laughs…' All right then, the next time I meet him, I'll laugh for three-quarters of an hour… I'd like to see him finished… dead! (*Hands the folder to* MARTHA) Here, you carry on…

MARTHA: 'They say of her that she's too feminine to be a man…'

ELIZABETH: I beg your pardon?

MARTHA: '…and not feminine enough to be a woman…'

ELIZABETH: I'm a hermaphrodite! Elizabeth, Prince Charming!

MARTHA: 'Like all self-respecting monarchs, she loves funerals…'

ELIZABETH: All monarchs love funerals. All right. So what?

MARTHA: 'During the service, she drowns out the choir's top notes with her sobbing… '

ELIZABETH: That's because I suffer…

MARTHA: 'Then the very same evening she turns up at a feast twined round Essex, and waddling like a… *birrocha encalorada*… '

ELIZABETH: What does that mean? (*Snatches the letters from* MARTHA) *Birrocha encalorada*… I'd say that was some kind of insult. (*Looks intently at the sheet of paper*) O look, there's an asterisk here… O Egerton's translated it… how kind of him! 'Waddling… ' N-o-o-o-o! ' …like a she-mule in heat'!? 'Then she proclaims that she has bestowed the title of Earl Marshal on her lover in recognition of his acts of valour in the battlefield of her bed… ' (*Very very calm*) …This doesn't even touch me… Sarcasm is the lowest form of humour. A she-mule in heat!! (*Terrifying scream. She hurls chairs, stools, lectern. She kicks the horse, which rolls forward. She gets out the pistol, fires a shot at it. The horse returns to its position*) Stay where you are! If you don't stop, I'll kill you. It's moving. It's moving. (*To the horse*) Stay where you are!

She puts the pistol back in her bodice.

MARTHA: Don't go mad! Just because this man Foexen writes things that you say yourself all the time… and your language is much worse.

ELIZABETH: I love him and I can do as I please! (*She notices all the furniture overturned on the floor*) This place is like a bloody brothel. Tidy all this up, Martha! (*Change of tone*) Here I am dying for love of this wonderful brute who won't even deign to throw me a word… a letter… and all I hear in my head is his voice. And all I can see with my eyes are his eyes… I am dying of love… I love him.

MARTHA: Come on, Elizabeth. Come on. It's all right. It will pass.

ELIZABETH: How many times do I have to tell you? I don't want it to pass. You and your 'It will pass.' (*Imitates her voice*) I like dying of passion. (*She touches her breast in the spot where she replaced the pistol*) O my God!

MARTHA: What is it, dear? Do you feel ill? Your heart? Sit down.

ELIZABETH: No, it's the pistol... I stuck it down here... in my bodice... it's slipped down... it's going to go off...

MARTHA: But it's empty. You fired it just now.

ELIZABETH: It's got two barrels... the second one is still loaded... it's primed... the trigger's cocked... it's going to go off... Jesus! I'm going to shoot myself!

MARTHA: Stay calm. Stay calm. Now I'll unlace your corset. Get up slowly. I'll have to start at the waist. Stand on this stool... Where do you feel it?

ELIZABETH: This is terrible! (*She gets on the stool very very slowly, moving with great circumspection*) Why do you have to make me get up so high to die... I'm on my tomb already.

MARTHA: There. Now it's unlaced... We'll have to slide it round under the armpit so we can get it round the back... Hold on while I get someone to help me... (*Runs towards the door*) ...Guard!

ELIZABETH: Are you mad? Look at the state I'm in... and you're going to let just anyone come barging in...

MARTHA: It's your choice, dear: a bullet in the stomach or an indiscreet guard?

ELIZABETH: A fortune teller once warned me I'd have trouble with a cock... I never thought it would be my own cocked pistol!

MARTHA *comes back with two* GUARDS.

MARTHA: Now be careful! You could set it off... we have to ease it round to the back...

ELIZABETH: Two of them? Why didn't you call the whole garrison? Bitch!

The three of them set to the task of getting the pistol.

MARTHA: Be brave... now you two... stretch your fingers... here... can you feel the pistol?

ELIZABETH: (*Looks at both young* GUARDS *with interest*) Good morning! Of course... Come on... feel it... touch it... run your hands over it boys... (*Change of tone: menacing*) If you make me go off, that's it... If I survive I'll murder you!

MARTHA: Now be good, Elizabeth... O damn...

ELIZABETH: There, I knew it... it's slipped down... It's here, over my stomach...

MARTHA: No, it's all right... It's even better... come on, we just have to turn...

The two GUARDS *are now behind the* QUEEN, *continuing the search.*

ELIZABETH: Hey, go easy... those happen to be my buttocks... O my God... (*Languid*) ...Oh. Oh. You might at least throw me the occasional affectionate remark... ! Louts!

MARTHA: Once more... come on, it's moving... nearly there...

A shot goes off.

ELIZABETH: O God! Martha! I've assassinated myself! (*Terrified*) Blood... I can feel blood running down my legs... O God... I'm dying... My Essex... I want him here... now... Robert! I want to see him for the last time.

MARTHA: (*To the* GUARDS) Out! Go away! Get out!

The GUARDS *leave.*

ELIZABETH: Shot in the arse... What an inglorious end for a Queen! ...Listen, Martha: say that you did it... Take the blame. (*Reaction from* MARTHA) I know they'll cut your head off, but the Catholics will make you a saint! Saint Martha-the-Arseshooter.

MARTHA: Let me see... (*From behind* ELIZABETH, *she lifts her skirt*) ...Help me: come on, lift your skirt up. I can't see any blood...

ELIZABETH: Are you sure?

MARTHA: No... there's a hole... but it's in the dress.

ELIZABETH: (*Melodramatic*) So that means the gun went off into thin air, and I've pissed myself... I have, Martha... (*Gets down off the stool*) ...and such a lot! O it's too humiliating! The guards pawing me off-duty... the pistol going off... pee all over me... (MARTHA *goes off and comes straight back with a basin and a towel*) ...and Robert doesn't love me any more... I want to see him... (*Snivelling*) ...Martha, go and find him for me... tell him to stop planning attacks on me... tell him if he'll come back I'll give him back the monopoly on the sweet wine...

MARTHA: Yes, yes, dear... I'll find him for you... I'll bring him here... First of all, come here so I can wash you.

ELIZABETH: (*Takes the basin from* MARTHA) Leave me be. I can manage on my own... You go on... Look for him... But don't tell him that I sent you...

MARTHA: Well what shall I say then?

ELIZABETH: Tell him I'm ill... that I'm dying... Yes, that's it... I've shot myself with a pistol... but don't tell him about the pee... for God's sake. (*She goes out, puts down the basin and shouts*) Martha, stop! (*Re-enters*) I can't let him see me looking like this. I just caught sight of myself in the big mirror! ...It gave me such a shock! Where is my little mirror... I want to see if it makes any improvement. (*Looks in the small mirror*) No improvement. No improvement at all. Martha, why have I grown so old these last thirty-five years? ...I can't let him see me like this... like a wreck... just so he can call me a 'crooked carcass' again... no, I can't... I'm ugly, horrible, old... (*She's stuffing little leaves into her mouth: she takes them out of the pocket of her dressing gown*) ...I'll kill myself ...O what a life!

MARTHA: Well to begin with, you can spit out that disgusting mess of leaves...

She goes to get a basin.

ELIZABETH: They lift my spirits... make me feel better...

MARTHA: They knock you out is what they do… and they make your teeth turn black so they look rotten… come on, spit them out!

She offers her the basin.

ELIZABETH: No I won't spit them out.

MARTHA: Come along, otherwise you'll have breath that stinks like a captive dragon's! Spit!

ELIZABETH: (*She spits in the basin*) A captive dragon's breath is just what I need… I've already got the skin… if I bumped into Saint George, he'd use me for target practice.

MARTHA *takes the basin off and comes straight back.*

MARTHA: Yes that's right… come on now, why don't you do something to pick yourself up a bit… a nice astringent poultice… a good massage to tone you up…

ELIZABETH: Not again… Not that old hag again… what does she call herself?

MARTHA: Dame Grosslady… yes, she's the one… the only one who can save you…

ELIZABETH: Yes. Save me with dung… that's what that old hag puts in those miraculous poultices of hers. She's disgusting!

MARTHA: Don't talk nonsense. What do you mean, dung? It's organic mud. Decomposing matter and putrified vegetable detritus.

ELIZABETH: There you are. You said it! The scientific definition of shit! Yes, I've been told all about her: she comes and slaps these poultices of organic dung – that's what you call it – on you; and you look younger – twenty minutes younger at the most… and in return you can't go out of the house because of the filthy stink you give off… so people say: 'Ah, doesn't she look young!' …and then SMACK! Out cold. For the love of God. And then I've been told, to lift the skin on your face, she pulls your hair back so hard you end up looking like a skull. A young skull, but a skull! And then she massages with her great meaty hands, she wrings your fat... and thumps you...

MARTHA: I understand. You don't feel like it... You're right. All that torture, and for whom? We won't bother...

ELIZABETH: (*Decisive*) Yes, we won't bother. (*Same tone of voice*) Go and summon Dame Grosslady straight away.

MARTHA: Yes but... hold on a moment...

ELIZABETH: Obey me!

MARTHA: You won't change your mind and make me send her away like you did last week?

MARTHA *goes and fetches a cloth.*

ELIZABETH: I told you to obey me... Damn chatterbox... how did I end up living with you? ...What are you doing now?

MARTHA: (*Pointing to the wet floor*) Wait a second, let me mop this up.

ELIZABETH: Have you gone mad? It's holy piss. I did it. I am the Pope. Shift yourself!

MARTHA: All right. Shall I bring her in then?

She goes towards the door.

ELIZABETH: Bring who in?

MARTHA: Dame Grosslady. She's waiting outside.

ELIZABETH: Already? How on earth did that happen?

MARTHA: I thought it might be a good idea. I sent for her.

ELIZABETH: Stop! Just a minute! Wait... I'm not ready... I'm afraid...

MARTHA: Just think of all the agony a hen has to go through just to lay an egg... Why, you'll be able to produce a new Queen! (*She goes to the door and shouts*) Open the door! Send Dame Grosslady in!

A gigantic woman comes in. She's wearing a white mask – a Venetian domino: DAME GROSSLADY. *She has a basket on her arm and other objects.*

GROSSLADY: Maxima domina te exelle nobis...

ELIZABETH: Stop right where you are! What's this mask you've got on?

GROSSLADY: I apparel it pimply to misguise the brutissimo mush undersotto it, Your Ladleship.

ELIZABETH: Take it off at once... I like to look people in the face.

MARTHA: What difference does it make? She only does it to help you. She doesn't have a very savoury reputation. If anyone found out that you used her to fix yourself up... her, next best thing to a witch...

ELIZABETH: I said the mask has to go!

GROSSLADY: God wot thee won't be squittered, Your Madge. (*Takes mask off*) Allora, ecco the vero me.

ELIZABETH: Dieu sauve moi, qu'elle est horrible!

MARTHA: Je t'avais prévenue.

GROSSLADY: Dinna fadge with the parleyvoo frog... I be perfetto conversazione in frog, signora magnifica. Si, I sembro a bloke, I savvy, a clapper dudgeon... and not too graziosa or snoutfair... Per favore, dinna facket me to feel blushful... And dinna be fritted of me, sweetling Queenie. I be a bona pimple copesmate, and I be come to aid and abatter you.

She goes to the door and pulls in strange wooden contraptions.

ELIZABETH: I certainly hope so, my dear Dame Grosslady. (*To* MARTHA) What language is this loony speaking?

MARTHA: How should I know? Sounds like a mish-mash of slang and some dialect or other...

ELIZABETH: And what is this round contraption?

GROSSLADY: Questo rattletrap we calliamo a strutter or stroller... and we serve it to apprentice you to trot on bawdyshoon without going tumblyshanks arsy-versy.

ELIZABETH: Bawdy shoon?

GROSSLADY: Take a squint. (*Shows her two things made of cork and skin*) Pattens con sole mios altissima three footsies.

ELIZABETH: Why don't you just call them stilts and have done with it?

GROSSLADY: The bawdybaskets in Venezia apparel them to look Monty-Blancy and skinny malinky.

ELIZABETH: Did you hear that, Martha? What a career I've had. From a Queen to a whore! Happy at last.

GROSSLADY: But Your Madge, those bawdybaskets pocket piles of loot.

ELIZABETH: I don't need to look any taller. I am fine the height I am.

GROSSLADY: Queenie, ifn tha preferishies we can leaviamo thee thus with a bucket of lard for an arse.

ELIZABETH: Really! What language. I can kick you out, you know.

GROSSLADY: Dinna fash thyssen, Magnifica... (*She slips*) Ooops a daisy! What hath I glissaded sopra? ...What be all this slipsloppy? Mayhap my peepers mistook me, but it doth semble like...

ELIZABETH: Yes... it was... my horse...

GROSSLADY: Hissen? A wooden prancer that pisseth? That be bona fortuna!

ELIZABETH: What do you know about anything? It's a royal horse.

MARTHA *and* DAME GROSSLADY *strap the clogs onto* ELIZABETH.

GROSSLADY: O marry then... The Royal Wee...

MARTHA: Be brave, Elizabeth, get up.

She moves clumsily on the clogs.

GROSSLADY: Bestir thyssen, Magnificence... Quetch! Opla! Quicketty presto into the strutter... (*They help her into it*)

...Bene ...That's the way to do it... Allora we shuttiamo thee in, snug as a bug in a rug... Assissta, assissta, Lady Martha.

MARTHA: Of course.

GROSSLADY: O guarda the Queenie! The bona lallies! Commandatore of tutto! Miracolo di largesse!

MARTHA: You look slimmer already.

ELIZABETH: (*Amused giggle*) In a baby walker at my age!

GROSSLADY: Does tha desideri a dummy to suck, My Ladle?

ELIZABETH: (*She doesn't react*) Don't I look rather ridiculous, stuck up here like this? I'm taller than my horse...

GROSSLADY: O dinna caparison thyssen to the wooden pisser.

MARTHA: Walk. Practise.

ELIZABETH: Take it from me, I'll learn to walk on these whores' clogs, and at the very first opportunity, when I meet the Portuguese ambassador, the 'mula encalorada' one, I'll fall down on top of him... I'll use him as a doormat!

While ELIZABETH *practises walking in the machine,* DAME GROSSLADY *brings on a dais on which she puts an armchair.*

GROSSLADY: Foot it, foot it, my sweetling beanpole...

ELIZABETH: When I'm in Essex's arms, as soon as he's given up these rebellions against me, won't he be amazed to see how tall I've grown... I'll ask him for a kiss... (*Laughing*) ...and he'll be kissing my belly button. (*Changed tone*) Get me out of this thing...

GROSSLADY: Beneship, beneship dearlie. Settle thine arse sopra this chaise the whiles I preparare the wrinkle-mousse to smoddle thee in.

MARTHA: Why don't you take it easy, and play your lute for a while. I'll go and fetch it for you.

ELIZABETH: No. Pass me those papers on the lectern.

MARTHA: The ambassadors' letters?

ELIZABETH: No, the manuscript of Hamlet.

MARTHA: Not that stuff again.

She brings the manuscript to ELIZABETH.

GROSSLADY: O. Omelette! I familiar him... I vide that at the Globule... Actored by that coneycatcher... quando whuffed out that... 'Scarper! Scarper into a convict house O-feel-a-me! Thy old man had been cozened and catched by thy bawdy parts else! Capricornified...! Scarper into a convento...!' Ha, ha, ha, ha...

She gets a jar out of her basket and mimes spreading cream on the QUEEN's *face.*

ELIZABETH: Do you always laugh like that?

GROSSLADY: Nay, nay, my voce be a bit ginger beer just now.

ELIZABETH: What is it you've put on my face? ...It's pulling my skin.

GROSSLADY: Flowers of fartleberry.

MARTHA: What on earth are you looking for in that manuscript?

DAME GROSSLADY *makes little plaits out of the* QUEEN's *hair and then ties them together at the back.*

ELIZABETH: The proof that this hack isn't writing just to make a fool of me; but that the brains behind Robert Devereux's plot are here!

MARTHA: What are you saying? That *Hamlet* is a piece of propaganda against you?

ELIZABETH: Martha, don't make fun of me. (*To* DAME GROSSLADY) And go easy you, you're not skinning a rabbit...

GROSSLADY: It be perfetto normalo, My Leeryship.

ELIZABETH: Listen, get it into your head, will you...

(MARTHA *takes the clogs off* ELIZABETH.) ...I'm not talking nonsense. This entire work is a fiendish attack on my person and my politics. This thespian guttersnipe is slandering me every single night at the Globe.

MARTHA: Listen Elizabeth, I happened to be at a performance of *Hamlet* at the Globe a few days ago, and I swear I didn't see any attack on you. None at all.

ELIZABETH: You saw it, and you never even had a suspicion? 'The frog lay deep at bottom of the well, perceived the pail above her, circlèd by the light, and took it for the very sun.'

MARTHA: What are you talking about?

ELIZABETH: It's a quotation from Shakespeare.

GROSSLADY: Bellissima! How doth it trip? 'The froggie in the fundament of the well tort the arsehole of the bucket was the sole mio... ' Splendido!

MARTHA: Be quiet! The only thing I understand is that she's calling me a frog... The rest is as clear as mud...

ELIZABETH: But it's Hamlet himself who says that.

MARTHA: Are you sure?

ELIZABETH: He could have said it. Even if I made it up, that's the way he talks.

GROSSLADY: Ulrika! It be like tha vidis a defection in a puking glass! Arse about face!

MARTHA: Hold your tongue!

ELIZABETH: No, no... she's right... that's exactly what it is... a mirror image. Exactly!

GROSSLADY: Chop on you, biggedy show-off!

MARTHA: How dare you talk to me like that.

GROSSLADY: Shut thy clapper, pinchfart! Pickfords they stampers. (*To* ELIZABETH) Marry come up, I dinna ken where tha finds thy servitudes, Queenie.

ELIZABETH: To put it precisely, this cunning shyster William Shakespeare... in order to disguise...

GROSSLADY: Pluck off thy shift. Scoot thy duds.

ELIZABETH: Never. Absolutely not.

GROSSLADY: No need for blushful. We be tutti feminies. The solo erectus here be the pissing prancer.

ELIZABETH: All women. I'm not so sure… (*Looks closely at* DAME GROSSLADY) …I have my doubts about one of us three, my dear Dame Grosslady.

GROSSLADY: Naughty, naughty. Dinna abuse thyssen. Th'art a reet good looking femina yet.

ELIZABETH: I just don't feel like it.

MARTHA: I've got an idea.

MARTHA *goes out and returns with a kind of screen which she sets up in front of* ELIZABETH, *covering her body but leaving her head sticking out over the top.* ELIZABETH *takes off her dressing gown and shift, helped by* MARTHA *and* DAME GROSSLADY. MARTHA *goes off with* ELIZABETH*'s garments and returns with a large sheet in which she wraps her.*

ELIZABETH: As I was saying, Shakespeare, in order to disguise the obviousness of the political allusions… has simply reversed the sexes of the characters.

MARTHA: What do you mean?

ELIZABETH: I mean that he has changed the female characters into males and vice versa.

GROSSLADY: He be untowardly pranking a drag act: dressing up in the puking glass.

ELIZABETH: Yes.

MARTHA: Give me an example.

ELIZABETH: That's simple: I'm female… Hamlet is male…

MARTHA: Yes of course, because Hamlet is a parody of you. I was forgetting.

GROSSLADY: Oy, Mistress Minx, stop that pulling the lallies. Don't make a pish at her.

ELIZABETH: Take no notice of her… (*To* MARTHA)
…Now then, are you listening to me? I am Hamlet! Sweet
Ophelia is female… and my beloved Robert is male.
Hamlet's father has been assassinated… my mother was
assassinated. The ghost of Hamlet's father pursues him
night and day… likewise my mother has continually cried
through my dreams for vengeance.

GROSSLADY: Vide how it all balenciagas out? Tat for tit.

ELIZABETH: Hamlet's mother marries her brother-in-law…
And my father too, Henry VIII, married his brother's
widow. That is, his sister-in-law.

GROSSLADY: Che famiglia hotch-potch…

ELIZABETH: It is my own story…

MARTHA: Wait a minute, don't cheat. Your father was
personally responsible for Anne Boleyn's death… but
Hamlet's mother is innocent.

ELIZABETH: Who told you that? Read the text carefully…
The Queen plays innocence, but Hamlet finds that she's
guilty… And my father Henry was the same… he
pretended to oppose the lords who condemned Anne
Boleyn to death. O you should have seen him raving and
weeping tears of blood over my mother's headless corpse…
Just like Hamlet's mother!

GROSSLADY: The puking glass imago! Esattamento!
Esattamentissimo!

MARTHA: Elizabeth, I'm sorry, but really you're carrying on
like one of those barrow boys who sell glue that's supposed
to stick anything to anything. I'm sorry… Tell me this: what
straightforward concrete reason have you got for saying
that you are Hamlet in the play?

GROSSLADY: Rispondo mio? But this be the finale time,
mark you.

ELIZABETH: Go on, try. We're listening.

GROSSLADY: Allora, Queenie here, Lizzie of Angleterror, it
be advised abroad, be possessed of a shockissimo

obfuscation: videlicet: when she vidis curtains or
tapezzeria stirring... she semper hath an excalibur to
hand... 'A bogey!' she brabbles... 'Thwack!' ...And devil
care who may be prinking behind.

She mimes running someone through.

MARTHA: Well yes, actually she nearly had me this morning.

GROSSLADY: By my troth, and she never poniarded thee?
Queenie, tha must needs practicare a bit more... Fancy
missing this doxydell... Anyroad up, Omelette hath this
same obfuscation... There be a scenario wherein the
tapezzeria stirs and Bolonius be dietro...

ELIZABETH: Polonius, who represents my chief councillor,
Cecil.

GROSSLADY: O what an allergy! Disna tha vidi? Dunque:
here we haviamo questo Bolonius who be the allergy for
Cecil, and he be dietro a tapezzeria, and here be Omelette
parleying to his mummikins, prating her the mostissimo
hoggish rude: 'How couldst tha matrimonial that pelting
pinchfart – thou dishclout!' ...Si, si. That be his modus of
parleyvoo to her. And then at a certo momento the arras
stirios... AAARGH!! A rattus! Thwack! You savvy, overby
in Lurpak-land, they have rattuses five and a half feets
alto... five feets nine at least. SPLAT... Stab with the
excalibur! THUNK! She jerrycumumbles him! Bolonius
the allergy thrummed on the parterre. (*To* MARTHA)
And the proxy allergy be thee...

MARTHA: (*To* ELIZABETH) O, you see, what a brilliant
proposition... Irrefutable!

GROSSLADY: Ah, tha doesna accordian with me? Okey
dokey, I must needs presentarey thee a secondo examplo.
At the finish of *Omelette*, who trolls up to puttiamo some
orderaro dentro the shit heap?

MARTHA: Fortinbras.

GROSSLADY: Shortinarse of Doorway. Bono. And who, so
the puritani whiffle it abroad, be the Shortinarse from out

the northo who will puttiamo some orderaro dentro the shitheap we calliamo Angleterror?

MARTHA: James.

GROSSLADY: Jams of Sconeland, perched on Hadrian's wall pronto to crash down on thy bonce, Queenie.

She gives a violent tug to the QUEEN's *head.*

ELIZABETH: Just be careful there, Dame Grosslady, you're the one who's crashing down on my head.

GROSSLADY: It be pimply on account of I be all eager beaver.

ELIZABETH: You're pulling my ears and eyes back so hard, I'll end up looking like... a mongol!

GROSSLADY: Pish! Mongrel! Thee comes up bellissima... Guarda, I've completamente disappeared thy bubble chin.

ELIZABETH: How dare you. I have never had a... double chin...

GROSSLADY: Tha be correcto. Tha had a bubble neck.

MARTHA: You must forgive her... she was getting mixed up with Hamlet. He's the one with the double chin... and the little pot belly... and the flat feet.

ELIZABETH: The subtle irony of your remark quite escapes me.

GROSSLADY: I comprehensived it! Shall I explicare?

MARTHA: No. Be silent!

GROSSLADY: Nae. I will story it to her. The nub is: the thesp who actors Omelette be nominato Richard Garbage. I savvy him bene. A cove of forty-two... under a bono lamp he doesna sembra a day beyant sixty-two... sixty-four... He be a thumping great pudding... moltissimo wheezing... and peach time he actors, he attracts an ashma... and in the duello with Layherpes – Layherpes be molto juvenilia, he flipflaps, he jumpers great saltos. Vidi what Richard Garbage fadges in the duello... he twiddle twaddles... he knits... (*She mimes knitting*) ...so at a certo punto... though he be never shifting... he whoofs out 'Arrgh, arrgh,

arrgh'. (*Panting sound*) And the Queenie dickets him 'O Omelette, tha's no a bairn nae more... Tha be brething through thine arsehole.' Shakespeare, eh? But they censoried that pronto... but that be what he scrivened... Allora, this Garbage be covered in sweater...

MARTHA: (*Interrupting her*) Covered in freckles too... and he's not got one, but two double chins... and he waddles and minces around halfway between a hen and a Muscovy duck.

GROSSLADY: Si. That be veritabile. He be all sidlewry. He trips all arsey versey with his trotters turned out. But when he actors... such forzio, he drunks tutti the spectatori...

She acts out in nonsense talk – grammelot – the soliloquy, 'To Be or Not To Be...' with all the intonations of a dramatic recitation.

GROSSLADY: And tha comprehensives tuttithing he parleys... he be a forza of natura... even though he be a bit campy fribble.

ELIZABETH: A bit? He's an raving pansy.

MARTHA: Well it doesn't show.

GROSSLADY: It vidies, it vidies... It lacks him but the plumes cultivating out of his arsehole. And forwhy did they presentare the part to this Monsieur Mingo de Mousetrap? There needs be five other tractors in the compagnia who had made a buonerer dog in a doublet... juveniler, spindlier, fitter tractors... and perche did they choosie this ham barm cake?

ELIZABETH: They chose him deliberately. A sour old clumsy has-been... They did it deliberately so there could be no mistaking that he's supposed to be my exact double... 'Queen of shining beauty... ' That's what those creeps at court say to me; and all the while my face is crumbling away... 'Goddess of Youth and Freshness... ' and I'm falling to bits.

GROSSLADY: Marry, tha canst not dickct that nae more. Not for thy mush anyroad up. Tocca how thrumming it be.

She gets ELIZABETH *out of the armchair and takes it off the dais.*

ELIZABETH: What are you up to now?

GROSSLADY: We must needs slenderise thy tripes and trullibubs, musn't we?

ELIZABETH: Tripes? What filth have you got this time?

GROSSLADY: Slugslurpers.

She shows her a jar she's taken out of the basket.

ELIZABETH: Leeches?

GROSSLADY: Nay. Leechies suckie gore. Ye grubbies suck blubber. Oooh... suck like... Guarda how bellissima they be... and the teensie blue sparklers... perky little capons...

ELIZABETH: They're disgusting. No, no. For heaven's sake. You want to put those revolting worms on my stomach?

MARTHA *makes* ELIZABETH *stand on the dais while* DAME GROSSLADY *puts the 'slugs' on different parts of her body.*

GROSSLADY: Si. And the hams and haunches also.

ELIZABETH: O for God's sake!

GROSSLADY: And the boulders, and the smiters... and the widow's hump dietro thy neck.

ELIZABETH: O God, I'm going to vomit.

GROSSLADY: And thy kidney-platz and thy botty. They'll slenderise thee dimber damber... Guarda the beasties! Guarda this little oinker! Attila! Caligula!

ELIZABETH: All right. Get on with it then. Just don't let me see them. Where were we?

MARTHA: Old Hamlet with his pot belly.

ELIZABETH: Yes, and he's probably impotent as well. He goes around saying he's turned on all the time, but he never does any fucking...

GROSSLADY: By my troth, such vulgaritude! The F-word

from a Queenie. And difronto of ye timidi little sluggles. Guarda this one. He's gone tutto pallido… Slurp away, Genghis.

ELIZABETH: But the thing that really gets up my nose is the way this bastard slanders me, saying I'm bringing the country to ruination. His: 'Something rotten in the State of Denmark' …What he means is my sewer, here, in England. Don't you see? Denmark! Who does he think he's fooling?

GROSSLADY: Ah, now I comprehensive this whole puking glass imago business… Quando he dicket: 'Lurpak-land be a dungeon' he intends: 'Angleterror be a dungeon… '

MARTHA: You've got doubles on the brain!

ELIZABETH: Is that right? All right then, listen: what happens at the end of Hamlet?

MARTHA: A massacre.

GROSSLADY: O si. At the finale there be dead corpuscles here there and tupperware. Layherpes excalibured par ici, the arsenickèd Queen par là… the King shite-ing through his denturas ici, Omelette gasparding his ultimo breathe par la…

ELIZABETH: And whose fault is it?

GROSSLADY: Omelette's. We all savvy it be Omelette's salt on account of he canst not make up his nous box. He dithers and dathers… He oughter've sorted it all long since. Excalibured the poxy nuncle pronto when he was down on his mary-bones jabbering prayers in the gospel shop. 'Now I'll excalibur him… no, half a mo' …dicket to hissen… 'I'll be doing him a flavour… cos he'd mort scusied of tutti his sins, and he'd locomote diretto to paradiso… My old man morted stuffoed full of sin and Boom!, locomoted to hell… I'll attend till nuncle locomotes into the chamber with mamma mia and they start playing at rantum scantum' …And then he sorties the excalibur… 'No, I willna fadge it today… tomorrow… we'll see… day dopotomorrow… I dinna ken… mayhap next week… ' Odds plut and her nails, he oughter've ordinated the whole shebang in the primo scena when the bogey of Omelette's dad poppied up and dicket: 'O-o-o-m-le-e-e-tte... ' The bogey dad parleyed an echo like all proper bogeys... 'O-o-o-omle-e-e-ette... i-i-it... be-e-e-e-e thy-y-y-y-y nu-u-u-u-ncle... he-e-e-e-e be-e-e-e-e the-e-e-e-e a-a-a-a-ssa-a-assi-i-n... mo-o-o-o-ort hi-i-i-im... '

ELIZABETH: But if he'd killed the King in the first scene, then he wouldn't have been able to write a tragedy with five acts.

GROSSLADY: Mine arse on a bandbox for five acts... Then there be O-feel-a-me passing over... and then the nick ninny locomotes to Angleterror and retornaries... and then the duello... Phew! I preferishi things clear. One action but clear. Clearissimo. The bogey dad poppy up, dicket: 'Omelette, he be the villain... ' 'O be he? ...Okey dokey then... ' Sort the excalibur... 'Assassin' ...But noo. It be 'Now I thinkiamo I'll waiter a bit... I'll circumbendibus... I'll draggie the trotters... I'll do it one of these odd come shortlies... '

ELIZABETH: And isn't that what I'm accused of too?

She turns round suddenly and squashes the worms.

GROSSLADY: Noooo!

ELIZABETH: What happened?

GROSSLADY: Nay, tha buffle-headed blowsabella. The slugslurpers be all squished... quel desastro... Just like the finale of Omelette... Tha's squished the Queenie...

ELIZABETH: And isn't that what I'm accused of too... ?

GROSSLADY: Squishing slugslurpers? They be correcto.

ELIZABETH: No. Of not eliminating my enemies... of not doing anything... You know what the puritans accuse me of: 'The Spaniards are throttling the Dutch right on our doorstep... and I, fainthearted Queen, let them get on with it... the Irish are in open revolt, and I... instead of undertaking a proper scorched earth repression, hesitate, negotiate, fiddle around and keep changing my mind. I talk to the Pope who has excommunicated me, and I refuse to talk to the Protestants who have elected me to be their Pope... '

DAME GROSSLADY *is fiddling with* ELIZABETH's *ear.*

GROSSLADY: It be on account of tha be troppo genteel... Tha dost license them to prittle and prattle... If I were thee... WHACK!!

Makes a gesture of chopping off someone's head.

ELIZABETH: (*To* DAME GROSSLADY) What do you think you're up to, poking your finger in my ear?

GROSSLADY: It be not mine digit... It be uno of the grublets creepied into thy lughole.

ELIZABETH: Martha, help!

MARTHA: O, Holy Mary, get it out!

GROSSLADY: It isna culpa mia ifn the grublets like greaseball lugholes.

ELIZABETH: O my God, I feel sick!

GROSSLADY: I canna gripper him... O here he be... Ooop-la! Gotcha. Guarda how blubbered he be... bellissimi little peepers!

ELIZABETH: Damned hag... Get away from me... Get away...

GROSSLADY: Tutti the novelty grublettes parterre... ! Guarda...

ELIZABETH *goes off, followed by* MARTHA, *to get dressed.*

GROSSLADY: Ey, but guarda the pastance and beverage this one hath glubbered down before he snuffled it. So blubberchumps! And yet his sparklers be peepless. Alas! Poor grublette! Here hung that wibble I have wobbled I know not how soft. Where be your soupsucks now? Your slipslimes so slushful and sweatsweet? O well, so it goesio. I will c'cn hikc him off incontinent chez moi to my hubby.

He be a Capitano Birdseye. And quando I show him ye blubbered grublettes he'll be betwattled. He'll locomotor quick coarseyfishing. He'll sticky ye grublettes sopra his anglehooks and hurl them to the fundament of the brook... And quando they vidi ye blubbered grublettes... Entrare the codpieces! 'What grublettes!!' ...SCRUMP!! And this even we haviamo a thumping great codpiece to nosh. Ha ha ha. But if'n you think on't, we'll not be noshing cod. Forby the grublettes hath noshed the Queenie and the cod hath noshed the grublettes. So in vino veritas, we'll be noshing the Queen!! Mine arse but that be a frisking dab think, eh? Howzat for an allergy? (*Pause*) To dicket the verity, I didna trade up that little parabola. It be Shakespeare veritably. It be his think, quando he facket Omelette to parley: 'Your grublette be your only imperator for diet... Your blubberchumps imperator and your low life bugger be but variable servizio... Vidi how a Queenie may make a processione through the tripes of your low-life poverty man.' It be sufficiently to give thee the frighteners! Quel idea pot, that Shakespeare! Tha canst not think one think he hath not thinked before!

ELIZABETH: (*Behind the tapestry*) Dame Grosslady! It might be my imagination, but I really do have the feeling that I'm thinner.

GROSSLADY: Nay, nay. Veritablymenty, it be not thy imaginaziony, Queenie. Tha must needs be slenderised. Guarda how puffed and blubbered the beasties be from sucking at thee... sembra in the pudding club.

She shows her. Passing one of the worms round the curtain with her hand.

ELIZABETH: (*Still behind the tapestry*) Aaargh! I told you not to show them to me! Stupid bitch! (*Change of tone*) Listen, could you work another little miracle... on the breasts... they're like two dried up lemons.

GROSSLADY: Tha kleps that a 'little' miracolo!! An tha gies me tempo sufficienty I can resurrectio the dumpling bubbies... I'll gie thee twa titties so gollumpus, quando tha crosses thy strappers 'twill sembra a mantelpiece – tha canst rest a varse of floribundikins sopra and sprinkle them each matin… O che bellissima! Bellissima duds!

ELIZABETH *enters wearing a dress and a court wig and a suitable crown.* MARTHA *follows her.*

ELIZABETH: It's just a little something I put on for wearing around the house… How do I look? Do you think Robert will like me?

MARTHA: He will be stunned.

GROSSLADY: He must needs be bog-eyed… As I be, over thee and Shakespeare's double omelette!

MARTHA *and the* DAME *put the pattens on* ELIZABETH.

MARTHA: And me!

ELIZABETH: Ah, so I've finally managed to sow a seed of suspicion in that head of yours!

MARTHA: I'm more puzzled than anything… You know that if what you suspect is true, it means there's an organised conspiracy behind the whole thing?

ELIZABETH: Of course there is.

GROSSLADY: Marry come up, I dinna convocate. Odds bodikin! Revoluziony organizzato by thesps? Canst tha vidi them, tutti the tractors with their wooden excaliburs and their canoni stuffoed with talcum and mush powder? 'Pronto for the revoluziony! Stuffo the canoni! Fire!' BOOM BOOM!! (*She mimes the explosion of a cannon loaded with talc. Has a coughing fit*) Finito the revoluziony!

ELIZABETH: Really. These thespians are just the chorus. There's someone behind them, firing real bullets. And I'll prove it to you. Give me the manuscript of *Hamlet*, and I'll read you this monologue replacing the male with the female. Instead of 'Prince', I'll say 'Queen'.

'Why what an ass I am. This is most brave,
That I, the daughter of a dear mother murdered,

Prompted to my revenge by heaven and hell,
Must like a whore unpack my heart with words
And fall a-cursing like a very drab… '

EGERTON: (*He comes on with another folder*) Excuse me. Am I disturbing… ?

DAME GROSSLADY *goes towards* EGERTON *and makes signs at him to be quiet.* ELIZABETH *gets up and walks on the pattens.*

ELIZABETH: Quiet backstage!

She continues the recitation.

ELIZABETH: 'How stand I then, that have a mother killed, a father stained,
Excitements of my reason and my blood,
And let all sleep? While to my shame… '

EGERTON: Who is she so angry with?

GROSSLADY: (*Under her breath, but getting louder*) She be actoring the party of Omelette. He be a wibble-wobble ambodexter transvest; portas plumes in his arse, and he takes the pish fuori the Queenie…

ELIZABETH: (*Trying to interrupt* DAME GROSSLADY) 'Bloody, bawdy villain… '

GROSSLADY: (*She explains the plot of* Hamlet *to* EGERTON *in nonsense language – 'grammelot'*) …ecco the finale of Action One! (*To* ELIZABETH) Your Infernalship, it behoves me to explicary this to him on account of he doesna ken sweet F.A. from Omelette. He must needs be one of the Old Bill… Paolizia… (*Continues to 'explain' the plot of* Hamlet *to* EGERTON) …finale of the Quarto Action!

ELIZABETH: Hold your tongue, Dame Grosslady… !
'Bloody, bawdy villain… '

Behind ELIZABETH's *back,* DAME GROSSLADY *mimes the plot of Act Five.*

ELIZABETH: Give me your hand!

GROSSLADY: I be quasi finito Action the Fist!

ELIZABETH: (*To* DAME GROSSLADY) If you say one more word, I will summon the guards and have you thrown out.

'O most pernicious woman!
O villain, villain, smiling damned villain! ...It cannot be
But I am pigeon livered, and lack gall
To make oppression bitter... '

Why are you looking at me like that, Egerton? Do you think I've grown? (*Indicating the clogs*) You probably didn't know that you go on growing until you're seventy years old, did you! (*Serious*) Tell me something, if someone had the impudence to mock your Queen in like fashion, making a fool of her with such insults... what would you do?

EGERTON: Your Highness, who has dared to show such a lack of respect towards your person?

ELIZABETH: (*Hands the manuscript to* EGERTON) Here he is: name and surname... and the vile speeches, word for word. If you, my dear Egerton, went to the theatre a little more often... to the Globe, for example... this very evening... you would hear them being repeated.

GROSSLADY: Tha'd vidi that Omelette be a kinder dragging act... he fakes pun o' the Queenie... And he be clubbered in the fundament of a well, transvested as a frog, regarding the arse end of a bucket, and he dicket: 'O che sole mio bellissimo!'

EGERTON: This is impossible!

MARTHA: It's true. These crude theatrical guttersnipes are insulting her... and the audience applauds it.

ELIZABETH: And all you're interested in is setting traps for Essex and his bunch of useless idiots to fall into.

EGERTON: Can it be true that they're saying these kind of slanders at the Globe? Sheriff Golber is there every evening. He hasn't noticed anything. He never told me they were making references to you.

ELIZABETH: Is that so? My wooden horse has more brains and imagination than you and Sheriff Golber put together.

GROSSLADY: And he pisseth also!

ELIZABETH: Give me that manuscript. Listen to me Egerton, and try to understand the real meaning of what I'm going to read to you.

GROSSLADY: Nay, miladly, he doesna comprehensive...

She's referring to the astonished look on EGERTON's *face.*

ELIZABETH: Silence, Dame Grosslady!

GROSSLADY: But guarda the expressiony on his mush. He doesna comprehensive. There be nae sparkle in his peepers...

ELIZABETH: That's enough... Hamlet speaks: 'To die, to sleep... ' O, Dame Grosslady, I am reading Shakespeare here, don't interrupt.

GROSSLADY: I dinna interrupto – but he doesna comprehensive.

She makes fun of the perplexed look on EGERTON's *face.*

ELIZABETH:
   ' ...To die, to sleep –
   To sleep, perchance to dream. Ay, there's the rub;
   For in that sleep of death what dreams may come
   When we have shuffled off this mortal coil
   Must give us pause – there's the respect
   That makes calamity of so long life... '

EGERTON: I don't understand.

DAME GROSSLADY *is very pleased.*

ELIZABETH: Well done, that's right... that's a good line for you... keep saying it... Just throw it in every now and again. It helps me. Go on, say it.

EGERTON: I don't understand.

ELIZABETH: 'You don't understand? If it weren't for terror of the beyond, everyone would slaughter themselves!

Thousands and thousands of people would put an end to themselves... they would hurl themselves off high cliffs, or into the sea... or they would throw themselves into fire... '
Now say your lines again, please Egerton.

EGERTON: I don't understand.

GROSSLADY: So what be new!

She goes over to ELIZABETH *and glances at the manuscript.*

ELIZABETH: Well done! You don't understand? But it's perfectly clear, wouldn't you say?

'For who would bear the whips and scorns of time:
Th'oppressor's wrong, the proud man's contumely,
The pangs of disprized love, the law's delay,
The insolence of office, and the spurns
That patient merit of th'unworthy takes... '

You can check I'm not making any of this up, Egerton...

GROSSLADY: Ecco me, checking it punctilio dicky bird for dicky bird. I spy it finigraphically to vidi tha doesna inventory any...

ELIZABETH:
' ...who would fardels bear,
To grunt and sweat under a weary life... '

EGERTON: O yes. He's really got it in for us.

GROSSLADY: He'll squeeze our brains to a snivel!

ELIZABETH:
'But that the dread of something after death,
The undiscovered country, from whose bourne
No traveller returns, puzzles the will
And makes us rather bear those ills we have,
Than fly to others that we know not of?'

GROSSLADY: 'Tis terribil-ay! I comprehensive his stratagemical acts and monuments! Questo Shakespeare dicket to the rabblement: 'What do you fadge? Shift your ways! Go to! You perfect to be put upon like slaveys, like dumbo bruttoes – pimply on account of your terrorizzato of tripping off to hell? Arseholes! Dandiprats! Hell be here, here sopra terra... not underbeyant. Divven be frit. Be a bravery! Arise! Shuffle off this governo of turd. Batter it to a tripes!'

She begins to sing a revolutionary protest song.

EGERTON: (*Shouting*) You're right, you're absolutely right! This is an incitement to rebellion, to revolt!

GROSSLADY: Tranquil thyssen! Thy nous box will explosive else. 'Tis too gross to swallow all at a catch! Go at it piano piano...

MARTHA: Just a moment. Now I think you're going a little too far... I don't see any real incitement to rebellion in this. Perhaps a tendency towards a sort of ill-humour... discontent, let us say...

GROSSLADY: (*She mocks MARTHA's attempt to play things down – mimes a chicken laying an egg*) PLOP! The ovum of harmonia! And a teensy Paisley inside!

She mimes something small running away.

EGERTON: Come what may, Your Majesty, I will arrest him and close down the theatre immediately...

GROSSLADY: And then tha canst fire and brimstone it... A puff of wind... some ambulating sparks...

ELIZABETH: You will do nothing of the kind, Egerton. What you will do is make enquiries and find out whether this Shakespeare is part of the Earl of Essex's plot... then we will see...

EGERTON: I will set up an enquiry straight away.

ELIZABETH: While we're on the subject of enquiries, have you been able to authenticate that letter to James of Scotland? The one that according to you was written by Robert of Essex?

EGERTON: Your Majesty, I am mortified, but I am obliged to tell you that you were right: the letters have been found to be forgeries... even the seals were forged.

ELIZABETH: You've been able to conduct a thorough inquiry in so short a time?

EGERTON: No – we simply hung the courier who gave us the letter up on a hook… After a while he retracted everything… he admitted that it was all a libel he'd made up on the spur of the moment.

ELIZABETH: Perfect! You see Martha, in our country, the quality of justice is now strained, it hangeth balanced from a butcher's hook.

GROSSLADY: Bella! Bellissima! What a metaphorical! Shakespeare, Shakespeare… Shakespeare…

ELIZABETH: No, Dame Grosslady. It's not Shakespeare's, it's mine.

GROSSLADY: But 'twas Shakespeare's stylo!

ELIZABETH: Well I dare say it will turn up in one of his pot boilers sooner or later… He steals all of his best lines from me… Now what is it, Egerton? What are you hiding in that folder? Bad news, I would imagine.

EGERTON: It is proof, Your Majesty.

ELIZABETH: Proof of what?

EGERTON: That certain bands of Puritans are preparing to give aid to the plotters.

ELIZABETH: (*Amused laugh*) Ha ha… Your trap turning against you, Egerton? You dangled the bait of the Armoury so the plotters would be well armed, and Essex would be provoked into an attack… You intended to screw him once and for all. And now, bands of Puritans are snapping at the same line. Oh! It is great sport to see an Egerton preparing the powder, and then on account of the mistakes he has made, to see him hoist with his own petard… BOUM!

GROSSLADY: Ha ha! Bona! Shakespeare!

ELIZABETH: It's mine, Dame Grosslady.

GROSSLADY: And what dost Shakespeare e'er scriven of his own? What? (*Pause*) Tealeaf!

EGERTON: I am at a loss to understand your extraordinary satisfaction, Your Majesty. One might think you were savouring the prospect of our possible undoing.

MARTHA: He's right. You must be mad. You forget it would be yours too.

ELIZABETH: Alright, alright… I went a bit too far. Very well then, what is keeping you from stepping in?

EGERTON: Your Highness, at the moment they are all dispersed in small groups… we are waiting for them to join forces. We will attack them before they can reach the Houses of Parliament or the Palace.

ELIZABETH: Which Palace?

EGERTON: This Palace. Your Palace.

GROSSLADY: Dost tha no comprehensive, Queenie? Questi abscotchalators be furnished with the brass neck to come here and mort thee.

MARTHA: Exactly!

EGERTON: So, Your Highness, I feel, and Secretary Cecil is of the same opinion, that you would be safer in some other place than this.

ELIZABETH: In other words, I've got to make a run for it.

GROSSLADY: Afterwards that I've confectionated the mantelpiece with the varse of floribundikins for you to sprinkle…

ELIZABETH: Be silent!

EGERTON: Yes, You Majesty. The Lords of the Privy Council, and the Commons and Bacon above all, they all insist that you take shelter in Kenilworth Castle… You will be escorted under armed guard, naturally…

ELIZABETH: Under armed guard? Why me? What have I got to do with this? With my own eyes I have read dozens of abusive scrawls on walls in London these last few days… and in none of them have I seen incitements to rise against the Queen and skin her alive. What I have seen are insults and death threats primarily to you, Egerton... to Cecil... to the Lords... not to mention Bacon... According to the people, it is you are giving me ill council... to them, I am still their Good Queen Bess. Allow me to offer you a piece of advice: why don't you move, the whole lot of you, to Kenilworth Castle under armed guard... it's safer there.

GROSSLADY: Ah! Terribil-ay Queenie!

MARTHA: Elizabeth, you are pitiless. Tell me when you saw these scribbles on the walls? ...I know it's weeks since you've been out.

EGERTON: Quite. Unless, Your Majesty, you've been wandering the streets at night alone?

ELIZABETH: Dame Grosslady, pass me that cylinder. (*DAME GROSSLADY passes her a telescope which is leaning against the bed*) I've been out with this.

EGERTON: What is it?

ELIZABETH: (*Hands the telescope to* EGERTON) It was a present from the Venetian ambassador. It's called a telescope or spy-glass. Hold it up to your eye. It's an amazing contraption. Don't be alarmed.

EGERTON: It's extraordinary... (*Points the telescope to the back of the auditorium*) ...incredible how everything looks so close. It's remarkable! It feels as if you could reach out and touch those people down there.

MARTHA: Would you mind passing it to me for a moment?

EGERTON: O I'm so sorry... Of course... Please do... It would certainly be delightful to have some of these contraptions for the police.

MARTHA: It's stunning!

ELIZABETH: Of course. I've already ordered a trunkful for you. Then you can keep an eye on all the citizens, all the time: what they're doing, who they're with... even behind their windows, in their own houses... You can watch them in bed, making love... or even when they're on the jakes...

Watching everything! A truly modern state! The watchdog state!

GROSSLADY: (*She snatches the telescope from* MARTHA) O Jesu! I must needs vidi doublet. I canna credit my peepers!

ELIZABETH: What is it?

GROSSLADY: Down beyant. At the fundament of the frog and toad... It guardas like thy lambkin, the Pearl of Yes-sex, gorgioso, vero? They be arrivarying in processiony... with all his rabblement... some few spectatori be giving them the clap...

MARTHA: Give that to me... (*She looks through the telescope*) ...Yes... they're armed... they're waving... they're appealing to the people to join them.

EGERTON: Goddammit... we didn't expect them so soon. Excuse me... (*He takes the telescope from* MARTHA) ...let me have a look.

ELIZABETH: (*She snatches back the telescope*) The contraption is mine. I take precedence.

EGERTON: You are right. Pardon me.

GROSSLADY: (*She gets another, smaller telescope out of her basket and points it into the audience*) Grab a vidi, Queenie, grab a vidi... I be frit we be battered to dirt this time.

ELIZABETH: Where did you get that telescope, Dame Grosslady?

GROSSLADY: 'Tis mine. I fetched it from Venezia... they do market them sopra barrows in the piazza. A free peeper with every ten wooden gondolas! Secreto militare!

ELIZABETH: (*Looking through the telescope*) Look, there's another group crossing London Bridge. And more coming down the Strand from Temple Bar...

EGERTON: Excuse me, but I must leave immediately. I must find Hellington and prepare the counter attack.

GROSSLADY: I will companionate thee to the sorty.

ELIZABETH: Stop! You will prepare nothing whatsoever! The orders are: no one moves. Let them let off steam for a bit; let them enjoy the applause of the shopkeepers and market apprentices.

GROSSLADY: Bona dicket, Queenlie! At the primo whuff of explosionary cannon they'll piss theirsen wuss than thy prancer!

ELIZABETH: There is one thing I want you to do, Egerton… Go to Secretary Cecil and order him to send Sir William Knollys and the Lord Chief Justice to Essex with this message… take notes…

GROSSLADY: (*She has taken a pen and some paper from the desk*) I be pronto to takiamo notey. I will facket the scrivening, Your Burblyship.

ELIZABETH: (*Makes a sign of agreement*) 'We come from…'

GROSSLADY: Pull thy prancers… I must needs scriven the addressio.. 'To the Pearl of Yes-sex, Yes-sex House…'

ELIZABETH: I am sending two of the Lords to take the message… There is no need to write the address…

GROSSLADY: Your Queenship, ifn the lords miss their way… the messagio would go adrift… It doesna fadge o'ermuch to scriven the addressio.

ELIZABETH: Well, hurry up then.

GROSSLADY: 'To the Pearl of Yes-sex – to be meted into his veritable mitts…'

ELIZABETH: 'We come…'

GROSSLADY: (*She repeats mechanically*) 'We come…'

ELIZABETH: '…from the Queen…'

GROSSLADY: '…from the Queen…'

ELIZABETH: '…to understand…'

GROSSLADY: (*As before*) '…to blunderstand… French…'

ELIZABETH: Don't talk rubbish! '…to understand…'

GROSSLADY: '…to blunderstand…' Pull stop! Well, that be

translucent…

ELIZABETH: Why have you put a full stop. I didn't dictate that.

GROSSLADY: 'Twas the finish of the phrase.

ELIZABETH: It certainly was not. Go on.

GROSSLADY: Allora, bomber!

ELIZABETH: No comma!

GROSSLADY: Semi bomber!

ELIZABETH: No semi-colon!

GROSSLADY: Excommunication mark!

ELIZABETH: No. I said no! There is no punctuation there!

GROSSLADY: But now I must needs tornare ye pull stop into some other fadge, savvy? Preferishy a floribundikins sopra? A strangleman's noose? Sanctus Giorgio sopra his prancer?

ELIZABETH: Be silent! 'We come from the Queen to understand… ' O all right then… comma.

GROSSLADY: Bomber.

ELIZABETH: ' …why certain articles of faith… '

GROSSLADY: ' …why certo tickles i'faith… '

ELIZABETH: (*Obstinate*) 'Articles'!

GROSSLADY: 'Tickles… '

ELIZABETH: *Ar*ticles!

GROSSLADY: (*As one to whom everything is suddenly clear*) 'Ah! Tickles!' …I vidi the game now… (*Begins to write again*) …Ah! Ah! 'Tickles!' Ah! Ah!

ELIZABETH: 'Between you and your Queen… '

GROSSLADY: Another Queen?

ELIZABETH: No!

GROSSLADY: The same Queenie as previous! 'The Queen… the same Queen as previous… '

She writes.

ELIZABETH: No. They'll know that.

GROSSLADY: Must they needs guessy?

ELIZABETH: Silence! ' …Are at issue… '

GROSSLADY: 'A tissue of lies… '

ELIZABETH: (*Correcting her, repeating the word but emphasising the 'A'*) *At* issue!

GROSSLADY: (*As if to say 'It's the same thing'*) Of lies.

ELIZABETH: *At* issue!

GROSSLADY: Bless you!

ELIZABETH: 'And need to be… '

GROSSLADY: 'Or not to be that be the question mark… '

ELIZABETH: That's enough! And need to be addressed…

GROSSLADY: 'Dressed… '

ELIZABETH: *A*-dressed!

GROSSLADY: 'Ah! Dressed!'

ELIZABETH: Not 'ah'… 'and'…

GROSSLADY: 'Undressed… '

ELIZABETH: 'You shall have law… '

GROSSLADY: Ah! You shall have more. Ah! More tickles!

ELIZABETH *looks at her threateningly. She begins to write again.*

ELIZABETH: 'Justice and the law… '

GROSSLADY: Just as before. More tickles just as before.

She has got to the bottom corner of the paper and can't fit all the words in.

ELIZABETH: ' …Justice… '

GROSSLADY: 'Just a… just a… '

Turns the paper round.

ELIZABETH: What are you doing, Dame Grosslady?

GROSSLADY: There be no room remaining for justice!

She goes up to EGERTON *and re-reads the whole letter – including the punctuation, in nonsense language – grammelot.*

ELIZABETH: (*Tries to interrupt her several times, and finally shouts*) Dame Grosslady! Fucking cow! The signature!

GROSSLADY: Si, I scrivened that… 'Fucking cow!'

She gives the letter to EGERTON.

EGERTON: With your permission, Your Majesty. I will return later. (*Glances at the letter and turns to* DAME GROSSLADY) What language is this written in?

GROSSLADY: Stepnitalian! It be comprehensived by rebels everywhere!

ELIZABETH: Egerton, declare a twenty-four hour truce. As soon as the Lords have spoken with Essex, bring him to me. Thank you!

EGERTON: Of course, Your Majesty. I will bring you news as soon as possible.

Exits.

GROSSLADY: Ah Queenie, did'st tha no vidi the pallidity of Sir Thomas when tha recked him of the graffiti against his scurviness? I wager Cecil and Bacon be cacking their kecks.

MARTHA: Dame Grosslady, please… speak in a more seemly fashion!

GROSSLADY: I apprehended to parley filth by neighbouring Queenies… fucking cow!

ELIZABETH: Dame Grosslady, you heard… Robert will be here before long. He might even decide to come this very evening. You promised me some miracle or other for my breasts…

GROSSLADY: I can fadge it… But I must needs apprehensive thee… Perchance 'twill stingle a bit.

ELIZABETH: Sting?

GROSSLADY: Si, forby questi.

She holds up a glass jar.

ELIZABETH: What's in there?

GROSSLADY: Buzzies.

ELIZABETH: Buzzies? Do you mean bees? And what are you going to do with them?

GROSSLADY: Primo, Martha, take ye twig of sandalwood. That be to facket fumo. I cleave the open pottle, and the buzzies indentro, sopra the dumpling... Then I license a smidge of fumo dentro... the buzzie frantics a fury – and FATANG! He stabs thee! Then incontinent tha'll vidi the bubby to get all blubberful! Plumptious! Unplumping! Sillyconey!

ELIZABETH: You are completely mad... my breast swollen by a bee? Those animals really hurt.

MARTHA: What an amazing discovery! I would never have thought of that!

ELIZABETH: So why don't you let it bite your titty then if it's so amazing?

GROSSLADY: (*Referring to* MARTHA*'s flat chest*) Tha would'st need a gorilla sting for that mopsqueezer.

MARTHA: I don't have a Robert to cradle on my firm breasts, my dear. In any case, you can always say no. We'll stuff your bodice with cotton rags...

GROSSLADY: Si, we can certo stuffy the camisa with cottone – but it never be similar... Dost tha no ken the ancient posy: 'Titties of cotton sempre feel rotten'... ? And what if perchance Roberto should desidera to stroko thee? Anyroadup, a buzzie stab doesna pain o'ermuch... for that since I'll smurch a peck of honey and myrrh sopra the bubby to take off the hurt.

ELIZABETH: Are you sure they'll be really plump and firm?

GROSSLADY: Well... they willna sembra balloonios... but I can prometto thee them bellissima.

ELIZABETH: All right then… Let's get on with it! We might as well go stark raving mad while we're about it.

DAME GROSSLADY begins to get all her bottles and jars out of her basket.

MARTHA: Good girl! Come on then, Dame Grosslady.

GROSSLADY: Buona. Attend whilst I smurch on the honey and myrrh… Assista me.

She hands MARTHA a piece of sandalwood, signalling to her to light it.

ELIZABETH: Just a moment. How long is this swelling going to last?

GROSSLADY: O… tray days… mayhap five… it be dependable on how long we leave the stabbie dentro the bub.

ELIZABETH: I see. So if you pull the sting out after half an hour…

GROSSLADY: Nay, nay. Mezz'ora is troppo lungo. Tha'd sprout a bubby like a water melony. Cosi!

ELIZABETH: That's all I need!

GROSSLADY: Lambkin Queenie, prendy a buona inhale.

ELIZABETH: Robert, love of my life, I am doing this for you.

GROSSLADY: Go to't, Martha. Facket the fume.

She puts the jar to the Queen's breast.

ELIZABETH: AAAAAARGH! O my God, that hurts… !

GROSSLADY: Splendido! That be marveloso! It stabbed her Giovanni Robinson! Hurrah!

MARTHA: Wait, let me blow…

ELIZABETH: I'm going mad here… it's burning me…

GROSSLADY: Dinna give in, dinna give in… Majestical, I be fit to pose some camphor sopra.

We see her put down the jar full of bees:

ELIZABETH: That's enough, that's enough... pull the sting out...

GROSSLADY: Nay nay... A wee whiles more... attend my sweetling, dinna give in... guarda, guarda... it be blubbering up sudden!

ELIZABETH: (*Happy*) It's swelling, it's swelling! OOOOH! but it hurts!

MARTHA: Don't give in yet... think about how beautiful you'll be afterwards. I'd almost consider having it done myself. (*Pointing to the jar on the stand*) What's that bee doing in the jar?

GROSSLADY: O he hath mistook his stab now... he be morted. Attend the whiles I preparare another pottle... a novelty buzzie.

ELIZABETH: Wait... let me get my breath back, at least.

GROSSLADY: Nay, the bubbies must needs blubber up equaliter... so tha canst keep a squint on them... Tha musna have one to blubber up and up, and t'other rest as flat as a plancake.

ELIZABETH: All right... get on with it then... (*She stops, very embarrassed*) ...O MY GOD...

MARTHA: What's the matter?

ELIZABETH: (*Very ashamed*) I'm pissing myself again.

GROSSLADY: That be perfetto normale... that be what buzzie stabs always effect. Piss thyssen dry... we will accusiamo the pissing prancer... allora... here we go the secundo! (*She applies the second jar to the breast*) Doth he stab?

ELIZABETH: No, it's not stinging.

GROSSLADY: (*To* MARTHA) Facket fume... fume... (*Turns back hopefully to the* QUEEN) Doth he stab now?

ELIZABETH: No, it's not stinging.

GROSSLADY: O thou buffle-headed buzzie! Tha doesna desideri to stab, eh? I'll apprehend thee a lezione.

She shakes the jar.

ELIZABETH: (*Preoccupied*) What's going on now? Am I going to be left with one breast swollen up like a melon and the other one like a dried-up lemon?

GROSSLADY: Nay nay... Guarda... I've clapped Macnamara, the Vengeancer.

She gets another jar out of her basket.

ELIZABETH: What's that?

GROSSLADY: An Irish hornetto...

ELIZABETH: An Irish hornet? (*She stands up*) O now I understand... You're in on this plot... You want to kill me with hornet stings!!!?

GROSSLADY: Dinna be frit, sweetling splendiforousness... it hath a stab more delicato than the buzzie... Now, now, dinna agitational thyssen.

Without realising what she was doing, MARTHA *put the taper on the chair when* ELIZABETH *got up.*

GROSSLADY: Grabble her, Martha!

MARTHA *pushes the* QUEEN *back on to the chair.* ELIZABETH *leaps up, shrieking.*

ELIZABETH: AAAARGH!! What's that? AAARGH! That's burning!

MARTHA: I am so sorry, my treasure... it's all my fault... I put the taper down there...

GROSSLADY: Gollumpus! Careless trapes! Firing the Queenie's fundament... (*Takes a basin*) ...Settle thee here, lambkin... settle in the basinetto... the acqua will colder thee.

In getting the basin, she inadvertently puts the jar with the Irish hornet in it on ELIZABETH's *chair.*

ELIZABETH: Get away... that's all I need, to get my backside soaking wet... (*She sits down*) AAAAARRGH!

MARTHA: What's the matter?

ELIZABETH: Did I sit on the taper again?

GROSSLADY: Nay... Now thee be settled sopra the pottle of buzzies... Addlepated buzzie! He didna desideri to stab thee on the bubbie, but he hath stabbed thee on the fundament... Catholico! Republicano! Scargillimus!

ELIZABETH: O my God! What a bloody mess! I've got one buttock like a melon, and one breast like a balloon, one titty like a dried-up lemon and the other buttock scorched... What a sodding state for a Queen to be in... And I'm still pissing myself...

The lights go down as the song begins.

SONG:

Elizabeth the Loony Queen

Loonie Lizzie took a fit
Said she wanted young girl's tits.
Wanted to be gorgeous, see
Had herself stung by a bee.

Had her titty stung, O cripes!
By a wasp with yellow stripes.
Knockers knocked, O rat-tat-tat-!
One is swollen, one is flat.

Refrain:

Mamma mia mamma mia mamma mia it don't half hurt
Mamma mia mamma mia mamma mia it don't half hurt.

One boob puffed up like a marrow
T'other flat as Harold's arrow
Waspie will not bite a bit
Will not bite the flabby tit
Will not take a bite of it.

Lizzie sat on that damned bee
Queen with one big boob to see
Had one buttock like a boulder
(This to stop her looking older!)
One boob up and one boob down
Bum lop-sided – don't she frown
Arsy-versy, what a fright

Then she pissed herself all right.
Refrain:
With one tit no, the other yes
The Queen does peepee down her dress.

Act Two
Scene One
SONG:

A Version of Isabella with the Red Hair
(Isabella La Rossa)

The prisoner from the tower is taken
Ah! Dear God, my heart is broken
Now my foolish life is over,
Gone for ever, gone my lover.

Isabella had three lovers,
Came to woo her red hair, ever,
The first one lingered near her door at night
The third came singing in the fading light
The other, hidden in her bed
Made love with her whose hair is red
Made love with her to give her pleasure
But now she will repent full measure.

Isabella, ah, don't do it
Now you're blushing, now you'll rue it
Making love with secret breath
Will bring this young man to his death
Your love is gone, young man so brave,
Love is a stone weighs on your grave.

Away, soon now the dawn will break
They'll kill you, hang you for love's sake
The first one lingered near her door at night
The third came singing in the fading light
The other, hidden in her bed
Made love with her whose hair was red
Made love with her to give her pleasure
But now she will repent full measure.

When the song Isabella La Rossa *ends, the lights come up very slowly. The* QUEEN, *centre stage, is sitting in the saddle of the wooden horse. She is looking through the telescope, which is pointed towards the audience. She is dressed as she was before: she has no wig on.*

To one side, clearly visible, on the tailor's dummy with which we are already familiar, is a sumptuous white ceremonial dress. On one of the chairs, a hooped petticoat, a cap, a dress. On the bed, clearly visible, a wig identical to that which ELIZABETH *usually wears.*

ELIZABETH: Are you still awake? Yes, yes. Those are your windows with the lights on. (*Into the wings*) Martha! For the love of God, Robert, that's enough! I can't take any more! (*Her voice getting louder and angrier*) MA-A-A-RTHA-A-A!

MARTHA *enters, running, and goes towards the bed.*

MARTHA: Here I am, sweeting. What's the matter?

ELIZABETH: Where do you think you're going? Can't you hear I'm not in bed?

MARTHA: (*Amazed*) What are you doing up there?

ELIZABETH: I got up here because it's the only way I can get to see Robert's windows.

MARTHA: Haven't you been to bed at all?

ELIZABETH: No! I can't close my eyes… I am all tense… like a drumskin!

MARTHA: Now then, dear, try to relax. Would you like some herb tea?

ELIZABETH: Herb tea be damned! Don't be such a fool. I can't close my eyes, I'm as tense as a drum because you've pulled back the skin on my forehead too tight. Look at me, stuck up here like a stuffed owl! Fetch the Dame.

MARTHA: Yes, straight away.

ELIZABETH: Tell her to bring something to cool my breasts down. They're boiling. You could fry an egg on them!

MARTHA: (*Upstage*) Get a move on, Dame.

DAME GROSSLADY enters. She has another basket with her.

GROSSLADY: Eccomi, lambkin… Che splendiforousness! Up sopra the pissing horse so betimes in the matin… She sits like a toad on a chopping block!

ELIZABETH: What have you got in that little basket?

GROSSLADY: Novelty hornybuzzies, carissima.

ELIZABETH: (*Terrified*) More? Go away, for the love of God. That last wasp sting felt like a stab wound… it's left me with a lump on my left breast.

GROSSLADY: Bona. We calliamo those Venuses bumpy d'amore… tha must needs cleave cunning to the prancer, we be locomotoring beyant.

She pushes the horse to the left.

ELIZABETH: Besides, you've made the breasts round, but they're very odd. They go up and down, up and down: they undulate!

GROSSLADY: O che meravigliosa Queenie! 'Tis a festive erotico… Blokes go berserko for that! Allora we pulliamo out tutti they pinnikins.

DAME GROSSLADY, helped by MARTHA – the two of them getting up on stools – take the pins out of ELIZABETH's hair, and undo the plaits.

ELIZABETH: Thank you. Just let me close my eyes before I expire… God! What a night I had! I feel so good! (*Change of tone*) Dame Grosslady, I feel dreadful! I had such a terrible night! During the night I heard shouts coming from Essex's house… it sounded like a pitched battle…

MARTHA: Pitched battle?

GROSSLADY: Nay, signora, there hath been no battaglia. I footed it hither and thither. I traversed the entire of London, truffling out buzzies… and my lugs harked nought

– not e'en the woof of a pooch... It hath been tanto
tranquillo, thou could'st have heard a bluebottle buzz...
Oh! The blowsy bluebottles buzzing in London yesternight!

ELIZABETH: But I heard gunfire too. Caliver shots.

MARTHA: It must have been a nightmare.

ELIZABETH: That's right. I had a nightmare: a terrible
nightmare! I dreamed about Mary Stuart!

GROSSLADY: Nay?!

ELIZABETH: Here. Walking around my room as if she owned
it... with no head.

GROSSLADY: Nay?!

ELIZABETH: And she was holding her head in her hands.

GROSSLADY: Extant? The noddle was extant? Come Saint
Johnnie the Baptist... Che prinking useful, what? Sans
mumping thy noddle, tha could'st vidi... (*Miming holding
a head in her hands and turning it round*) ...par here... par
there...

ELIZABETH: It was terrifying. The eyes moved, the mouth
spoke... it was laughing and sneering, saying: 'Filthy
bitch... Filthy bitch'.

GROSSLADY: O no!

ELIZABETH: 'Things have turned out bad for you, it's not my
head that's rolling, but Robert's! Ha, ha!' And then:
PRRRTH! She blew a raspberry at me.

GROSSLADY: A gobfart from the noddle decapitato!

MARTHA: O how dreadful!

ELIZABETH: And then suddenly she began to play with the
head like a ball... she threw it up in the air... and she caught
it. And then... boum, boum, boum, she was bouncing...

GROSSLADY: Trouncing?

ELIZABETH: The head!

GROSSLADY: Then che?

ELIZABETH: Then the head escaped from her and yelled 'Christ... you're killing me... I'm not a bloody football!'

GROSSLADY: God's blood and tonsils, the noddle was correcto! And par where be the Signora's noddle? She did cleave to it! Okey dokey. Smite me with a smicket, I comprehensive the intendio of this nocturnal emission... It intendios that ye Pearl of Yes-sex hath tossed his noddle.

ELIZABETH: (*Appalled*) What are you saying?

GROSSLADY: He hath tossed his noddle from amore... of thee.

ELIZABETH: Ah, if only that were true.

MARTHA: Yes, everything will turn out for the best, you'll see.

GROSSLADY: (*To* MARTHA) Whilst we parley-voo of amore, dicket her who be en voyage to vidi her...

MARTHA: O yes, I was forgetting... the ringleader of the conspirators will probably be coming here some time today.

ELIZABETH: Robert?

GROSSLADY: Roberto of Yes-sex hath confectionated his nous-box to come to thee to pay his respectuosos. Isna thee oversopra the moon?

ELIZABETH: (*Aggressively*) Why didn't you tell me this before?

MARTHA: With all this business about nightmares.. It went right out of my head....

GROSSLADY: Thee facket attenzione tha doesna locomotive out of thy noddle for real... tha savvies what arrivies to those folk... (*Mimes heads being chopped off and bouncing them like balls*) Trouncy! Trouncy!

ELIZABETH: Come here, Dame Grosslady, get me down.

GROSSLADY: Si, Your Infernalship.

MARTHA *helps her to get the* QUEEN *down.*

ELIZABETH: Put my hair up... Robert will be here before

long, and I want my skin to look smooth. And Martha, you keep watch with the telescope.

Knocking at the door.

ELIZABETH: Someone's knocking... don't let anyone in while I'm in this state.

GROSSLADY: (*Going to the door*) Dinna flitter thy twitters wi' banging. The Queenie isna making audience. She be all awry, and sembras an owl in an ivy bush. (*She peeps round the door*) Your Hellhoundship, it be the Chiefo Pig of the Old Bill... The spy-glass whisker splitter.

ELIZABETH: Egerton? Let him in. Perhaps he's bringing news about Robert.

GROSSLADY: Facket him entrare to vidi thy slubberdegullionness, Your Ladle?

ELIZABETH: Blindfold him.

GROSSLADY: Darkness the chiefo Pig of the Old Bill. That had given him a fart attack!

ELIZABETH: Pull his hat down over his eyes.

GROSSLADY: Buona intelligence! Entrare, entrare, Sir Thomas! (*Pulls his hat down over his eyes*) It be the Queenie's orderaro I must needs tweak thy titfer sopra thy peepers for that since... O damnwit! What a noddle! Your Leeryship, he hath such a mumping great noddle, it willna locomotive in the titfer... The executionaro woulds't twist his knickers o'er that noddle... ah, I arrivied... that be it. Off tha wends...

ELIZABETH: Help him down. Don't let him fall. I don't want him damaged.

GROSSLADY: There be many more mickles where he muckled from.

ELIZABETH: What news do you bring me, Egerton?

EGERTON: Your Majesty, I trust you passed a... (*He stumbles*) comfortable night...

ELIZABETH: I passed a terrible night! I wish to know why I have seen no sign of the delegation of Lords on their way to Essex's house. Why is that?

GROSSLADY: Rispondi the Queenlie, your boredship.

EGERTON: Your Majesty, Sir William Knollys was nowhere to be found, and as there was no one who could take his place, we thought it best to put it off until today.

GROSSLADY: Smoothie tongue bastardo!

She pushes horse back to original place.

ELIZABETH: Is that so? You propose, you dispose, and you say nothing of all this to me? What are you hiding in that folder?

EGERTON: I am mortified, Your Majesty, but I have to concede once again that your suspicions were well founded.

He opens the folder.

ELIZABETH: What suspicions?

EGERTON: This mountebank… (*Tries to read, squinting under his hat*) …what's his name… ?

ELIZABETH: Is he called Shakespeare?

EGERTON: Yes, that's it. He is the one… he is one of the company.

ELIZABETH: Which company?

EGERTON: Of conspirators.

GROSSLADY: Conspiratori? Shakespeare be a revoluzione? Well, that be a burn up for the hooks!

ELIZABETH: Are you certain of this?

EGERTON: More than certain, Your Majesty. This Shakespeare is some way or another dependent on the Earl of Southampton… besides which, Southampton is his theatrical patron, since he is joint owner of the Globe.

ELIZABETH: So what?

EGERTON: But Your Highness, Southampton is one of the ringleaders of the plot.

GROSSLADY: (*Gobsmacked*) Nay! Your Leeryship! Tractors and theatricals dabbledoing in politicko? Incredibile! What next!

ELIZABETH: (*Becoming more and more upset*) Southampton, my only living relative. I have always shown him affection and sympathy, and now he's joined those pigs who want to screw me... he must be mixed up in this business of the letters to James of Scotland too...

MARTHA: Now Elizabeth, keep calm...

ELIZABETH: BE SILENT! I'll kill them... I'll hunt them down from house to house... myself! I want them hanged! Drawn! Quartered! (*She can no longer control herself*) I want them left to dangle until they rot! I want to see all the birds in England flocking to rip out their entrails! I feel sick. Martha, I'm going to vomit.

She doubles up, holding her stomach.

MARTHA: There we are. I knew it... Come on, come with me...

They exit.

GROSSLADY: She be vamoosed. (*She lifts* EGERTON's *hat*) I'll elevate the titfer. Get a bit of a breathe.

EGERTON: I am so sorry to have been the cause of this extremity...

GROSSLADY: Thou wast fortunato tha didna cop the sparkle in her peepers... Something scutcher! ...Horripilant... just like her skin and blister, Bloodful Mary, when she made bonfires o' all the Prods... But there be no ho with her. She be a carroty pate... Like her dad, Henry the Carrot-Top... horripilant! An entiro famiglia of carrot-tops. All scutchers!

EGERTON: What are you babbling about?

GROSSLADY: There be a snotto in my land that locomotives: 'Red head at night, Henry's delight. Red head in the morn, prepare to be shorn... '

EGERTON: I feel sorry for Southampton. His days are numbered, poor man. And Shakespeare too...

GROSSLADY: THWACK!! The scrivener's noddle into the pannier also! Sir Thomas, dost thou savvy forwhy the English eternity boxes be tiddler than anyplace else?

EGERTON: No, why?

GROSSLADY: Forby in Angleterror, nearly all the omnumgatherum of folk be buried wi' their noddles in their mitts!

EGERTON: Very witty...

ELIZABETH *and* MARTHA *return.*

GROSSLADY: (*Swiftly pushing the hat back down over* EGERTON'*s eyes*) Divven laugh so broadcast. Here be the Queenly. (*To the* QUEEN) How dost tha go? Fitter?

ELIZABETH: Much better, thank you. Egerton: enough of this. I cannot take any more. I am sick to the teeth of these plots, these impudent plans... Do we understand one another, Egerton? How is it possible that every time one faction wants to eliminate another, they never fail to drag me into the middle of it? What has it got to do with me? I've had enough! I am sure that if you all set yourselves to it with goodwill, in a day or two we'll hear no more of this tangled mess! And, as they say in the theatre at the end of plays: all's well that ends well between the sheets of a nice clean double bed! (*She laughs, much amused*)

Excited shouts outside the door... The sound of running footsteps.

VOICE FROM OUTSIDE: Raise the alarm! Raise the alarm! ...There he is... Over there!

Knocking at the door.

ELIZABETH: (*To* MARTHA) What is it now? Go and see.

More knocking... more violent than before.

MARTHA: What's got into you? I'm coming! (*She opens the door a crack*) Just a moment...

GROSSLADY: It be the voce of thy Capitano of Guardi.

MARTHA: Yes, it's him. He says they've seen a man climbing up… Shall I let him in?

ELIZABETH: Let who in? Have we all gone mad? Let him into my bedroom first thing in the morning? The Chief of Police can deal with it… Egerton, search by all means, but do it outside my room.

EGERTON: (*Without raising his hat, sets off determinedly towards the audience*) With your permission… I will go immediately.

GROSSLADY: (*Blocking his way*) Stoppo! Here be a chasm! Dinna be previous into thy eternity box. (*She accompanies* EGERTON *to the door*) Your Impiousness, that snotto be verily, when it dicket 'When justizia be blind, pigs might fly…' Permetto the Guardi to entrare, Your Ladleship, there be grand perilsome.

MARTHA: She's right. If there really is an assassin around…

ELIZABETH: There is no assassin… it's all a charade to get the palace into a state of panic so they can prevent Robert from coming to me. But I'm not falling for it.

She goes towards the bed.

MARTHA: Or maybe it's because you want to stop them before they can poke their noses between your sheets? Tell the truth, have you got someone in the bed?

ELIZABETH: Shut up, you witch! (*Opens the doors of the bed*) Thomas… hurry up, wake up!

A YOUNG MAN *appears, half naked.*

MARTHA: O, Father Christmas has come early this year! How are we going to hush this one up?

GROSSLADY: Hust tush! It be more splendido than a Royal Waddling. I can vidi the bedlines now: 'Midnight Gurgler in Suckingham Phallus' …Dost tha no ken what has chanced? A miracolo extraordinario! In the wee small hours o' the matin, and it was yet nearly darkmans… infatto, it was darkmans… previous to the bunrise… Elizabetta's lugs harkied a weeping blightingale… CHEEP CHEEP… in the gardino… She locomoted downio… and remark! there be a wee birdie... CHEEP CHEEP... tutto froze... she catched him up – poor wee sleekit frozen timorous birdie... CHEEP CHEEP... and she laid him on her breastie... and she – Good Samaritan that she be – retornaried to her virgin couch and she laid him down betwixt the linen sheets and she huffed on him, and puffed on him with gentle gree... and WHOOSH! ...CHEEP CHEEP!...WHOOSH!! This young dimber damber upsprang! Incontinent the Queenly thumped herself down on her marybones... 'Santa Rosalia, the most bellissima santa of the lot... What should I facket with this young springer?' And the santa rispondida: 'Si. Si. Facket the springer and his dicky birdie!' And that be the truth the whole truth and nothing like the truth!

ELIZABETH: (*To the* YOUNG MAN) Thomas, wrap yourself up in this counterpane. (*To* MARTHA) Where shall I hide him?

MARTHA: Let him down from the window.

GROSSLADY: Bravo! Thus he'll be taken for the assassino... CHEEP CHEEP! He'll retornare back into a wee birdie!

ELIZABETH: (*To the* YOUNG MAN, *who is starting to get dressed*) Don't wait to get dressed, Thomas, there isn't time.

YOUNG MAN: Your Majesty, I can't go out like this... with the counterpane...

ELIZABETH: Go out? And let the guards discover that you've been with me?

MARTHA: Why don't you dress him up?

ELIZABETH: O be quiet!

GROSSLADY: Si, bravo! Drag him up bona in lady's togs. Bona idea.

ELIZABETH: As a woman?

GROSSLADY: Si.

ELIZABETH: (*To* MARTHA, *pointing to the clothes that are lying on the chair*) Give me those clothes. We'll pass him off as one of my maids in waiting. (*Gives him a pat on the backside*) You've got the pretty little bottom for it!

YOUNG MAN: It's not right for you to make a fool of me like this. Dressing me up in women's clothes!

ELIZABETH: Don't be difficult, Thomas!

YOUNG MAN: Don't make me, please! I'd rather throw myself out of the window just as I am!

ELIZABETH: That'll be good. That way everyone can go round telling each other how the Queen uses young men... She squeezes them dry and then throws them out of the window, stark naked! Get dressed. Go over there, come on. That's an order!

The YOUNG MAN *goes out, unwillingly.*

MARTHA: (*Referring to the* YOUNG MAN) Well, as Epicurus says, sleeping in the arms of young men does wonders for the complexion!

GROSSLADY: Thee be completo oversopra the toppo. Attenzione the noddle! Trouncy! Trouncy!

ELIZABETH: You are a hyena. I simply wanted to make an experiment. I wanted to see whether I was in a fit condition to bear the attentions of a man, in case Robert came.

GROSSLADY: The try-out springer! The titty tester!

ELIZABETH: What a disastrous night! A total failure! I couldn't bear to be touched anywhere. I hurt all over. You have wrecked me, Dame Grosslady. I should have said: 'Stop that! It hurts!' But I didn't like to, so I went: 'O noooo... Dearest.... noooo.' The cretin thought I was doing it out of passion and he jumped on me, he jumped on me! I could have killed him! And then he had the nerve to ask me 'How was it for you, your Majesty?'

GROSSLADY: (*Alarmed*) Your Margerine, there be a rapscallion... undersotto in the gardino... in the maze... the Guardies... be hollering and woofing after him with the pooches.

MARTHA: Who is in the maze?

GROSSLADY: It must needs be that bastardo who was essaying to climber-clamber dentro this chamber to mort the Queenly. Oops, he be over forby.

ELIZABETH: Run down... order them to bring him to me immediately, alive! (MARTHA *goes out of the main door of the room*) I want to interrogate him myself!

GROSSLADY: Alive-alive-oh! Thus afterward we can draggiamo him up as a femminile too! Ha ha!

ELIZABETH: Follow me, Dame Grosslady. We will go and watch from the terrace.

She goes, using the door on the right.

GROSSLADY: Let us go, hugger-mugger! What spice! One entire festivity here at court! A coup de theatre every minuto! From the burnt cinder tha canst vidi an abscotchalator chased by hounds... a young dimber damber starkers in the Queen four toaster... just like Niente Sex Per Favore, We Be Inglesi!

She goes out, following the QUEEN.

Almost at the same moment, the YOUNG MAN *re-enters. He comes from behind the bed, and is only half dressed as a woman. He has the petticoat on, but his torso is naked.*

YOUNG MAN: Your Majesty, forgive me... I just don't feel...

He looks round for the QUEEN. *A man appears from behind one of the hangings. It is the* ASSASSIN.

ASSASSIN: You imbecile, bloody little idiot. What the hell do you think you're up to?

YOUNG MAN: (*Amazed*) Who is that? O, it's you, father... The Queen can't be far away... and the whole place is swarming with guards.

ASSASSIN: Exactly. And you choose a moment like this, to make a fuss over a house dress and a woman's cap.

YOUNG MAN: But it's so humiliating!

ASSASSIN: Halfwit! What matters to you more: standing on your dignity or the success of our cause?

YOUNG MAN: Yes, but when they make you eat dirt... turn you into a drag act... degrade you...

ASSASSIN: Oh yes. Is that why you were cavorting in the bed of a murdering illegitimate bitch, letting her kiss and fondle you? She was slobbering all over you, you little gigolo...

YOUNG MAN: But you ordered me to let her take me to bed.

ASSASSIN: Yes but I didn't order you to enjoy it...! Never forget, Thomas, it is she who murdered Mary!

From outside there is more shouting and a few shots.

YOUNG MAN: (*Indicating the window*) Who's the poor sod they're chasing?

ASSASSIN: Poor sod, you call him? If only you had his courage! He's been creating a diversion so I could get up here undetected. Now, get a move on, it's time for you to do your bit. You have to stay in this room for as long as you can to cover me. As soon as we've dealt with the Queen, you will give the alarm. And you make sure you send the guards upstairs to the attics... I'll make my escape down below.

YOUNG MAN: Are you sure we should do it? The place is going to be full of people soon... I heard them say Essex was on his way.

ASSASSIN: No, Essex won't come here... he might attack.

YOUNG MAN: Attack? But the Lord Chief Justice went to fetch him in person.

ASSASSIN: Listen to me carefully, Thomas: if Essex comes here, he will only come armed to the teeth and accompanied by all his men... And behind them, the whole city will be rising... They will finish off Cecil, Bacon and half the Lords... But they will save the Queen... and we cannot allow that to happen... So get a move on... Get on with it. You'll do everything she tells you without making a fuss, do you understand? Even if she asks you to walk on your hands with a lighted candle stuck up your arse.

YOUNG MAN: O no, not a lighted one!

ASSASSIN: Shut it! I'm going to get in here, in the horse.

He approaches the animal's stomach.

YOUNG MAN: How can you get in there?

ASSASSIN: There's a little door here. Come on, give me a hand.

He lifts the saddle cloth and opens the horse's back part like a door.

YOUNG MAN: O look, an arsehole that opens!

ASSASSIN: This horse belonged to Henry, Elizabeth's father... he used to hide his lovers in here... my mother among others. No one knows about this hidey-hole, not even Elizabeth. Come on, give me a leg up. No, stop. I don't fancy getting into the horse. Put it back. I prefer the chimney. At the right moment, when the coast is clear, give me the signal. Blow a few notes with this flute. (*He hands him a short flute*) Come on, take it.

YOUNG MAN: All right, get a move on then!

ASSASSIN: Just be careful no one lights a fire.

He gets into the fireplace and up the chimney. More shots from offstage.

YOUNG MAN: Who'd want to light a fire. It's spring! Go on!

The QUEEN *and* DAME GROSSLADY *return.* ELIZABETH *is wearing full ceremonial dress, wig, crown, jewels, etc.*

GROSSLADY: I desidero to savvy how that bloke confectionated to mort hissen.

MARTHA *re-enters from the gallery.*

ELIZABETH: Martha, who fired?

MARTHA: He did... he shot himself.

ELIZABETH: The shot that was supposed to be for me. So now we'll never know who sent him. (*She notices the* YOUNG MAN *who is looking uneasy*) And what do you think you're doing still in that state? I'll have to let the guards in in a minute… that thug is sure to have an accomplice. Do you want to compromise me?

YOUNG MAN: All right, Your Majesty… I'll put on the whole dress.

ELIZABETH: No, wait. Put on this dress instead.

She points to the dress on the dummy.

YOUNG MAN: But that's one of your dresses, Your Majesty.

ELIZABETH: Martha, help him. I want to see what it looks like on. I have never worn it.

YOUNG MAN: Wouldn't it be better to put it on your Maid of Honour?

MARTHA *and* DAME GROSSLADY *dress the* YOUNG MAN*: dress, pattens, wig and crown.*

ELIZABETH: No, it isn't her size. Anyway, I want you to really experience what it means to play the part of a Queen. All you young braggarts just flit around like dragonflies.

GROSSLADY: Elevate thyssen! Elevate!

ELIZABETH: That's where I want you. How do you feel?

YOUNG MAN: Squashed, squeezed… It's hell. I feel so embarrassed. Please don't ever tell anyone about this.

Smoke begins to come out of the fireplace.

GROSSLADY: Elevate thyssen sopra these bawdy shoon.

ELIZABETH: What's going on? What's that smoke coming out of the chimney?

GROSSLADY: Odds plut and her nails! The handleprick hath tumblied into the furplace.

ELIZABETH: (*Takes a jug of water and flings it into the fireplace*) Put that damn fire out!

GROSSLADY: O, mountaineers of fume!

We can hear muffled cries from the chimney.

GROSSLADY: Queenly, I can catch screech-howls from the chimbley: hark to the screams! AAAAAAARGH!

ELIZABETH: Who is screaming?

GROSSLADY: (*Imitating the sounds coming from the chimney*) AAAAAAARGH! It be the chimbley. It be the voce of the chimbley.

ELIZABETH: Don't talk rubbish. No one's screaming.

GROSSLADY: It must needs be the Jenny Lind!

YOUNG MAN: Yes, yes. It's the wind.

GROSSLADY: Do they e'en torturare the Jenny Lind in Angleterror?

ELIZABETH: Be silent, all of you! (*Turning to the* YOUNG MAN) Adorable! Have you ever played girls' parts?

YOUNG MAN: No, never...

ELIZABETH: Do you know I maintain a company of boys?

YOUNG MAN: Yes, Your Majesty, the Children of the Queen's Chapel, I know them.

ELIZABETH: But not one of them makes such a believable girl as you do.

YOUNG MAN: Now you're making fun of me again...

ELIZABETH: No, not at all. I'm going to put *Hamlet* on here at the court... So I can find out what's behind it... and you can play Ophelia, and Dame Grosslady can play the Queen!

GROSSLADY: That thumping great blowsabella! Thanks but no thanks.

The ASSASSIN *gets out of the chimney trying to stifle a coughing fit and hides behind* ELIZABETH's *bed. More shots are heard in the distance.*

MARTHA: What's going on now?

ELIZABETH: (*Looking towards the back of the auditorium*) They're culverin shots... or... My God, they're coming from Essex House. They've broken the truce! Give me the telescope immediately! No, better still, I must talk to Egerton. (*Towards the door on the right*) Egerton? Where has he got himself to? (*To* MARTHA) Come along, we'll go and find him.

They leave.

YOUNG MAN: (*He has picked up the telescope and he is now looking out into the auditorium*) O how wonderful… ! Everything's so big!

GROSSLADY: (*She has discovered the flute left behind by the* ASSASSIN) O vidi! A piccolo!

She blows into it; tries to get a few sounds out of it.

YOUNG MAN: Christ! What are you doing? No! That's the signal! Give me that!

The YOUNG MAN *tries to snatch the flute out of her hand. At this point an 'incident' occurs: sound of flute music begins.* DAME GROSSLADY *makes signals to the sound operator. The music does not stop.*

GROSSLADY: The Magic Flute! Tha canst sound it e'en if tha doesna whuff in it! All tha needs do be dingle thy digits!

The music stops.

YOUNG MAN: Give me the pipe!

GROSSLADY: Give me a smacker in exchangio!

YOUNG MAN: No! Get away, you old hag!

GROSSLADY: Mio? Old hag? Tha kleps mio old hagslag? I would'st a bolt of blightning strike thee! CCRRRACHK!! (*She mimes a bolt of lightning reducing him to 30 cms*) As swart as that! Bawdy shoon and all! (*She goes off behind the bed*) Short-arse pygmy!

YOUNG MAN: (*Going to chimney*) Father? Not there. Let's hope he hasn't suffocated. (*Turns round to look through the telescope again*) This must be witchcraft! It's fantastic!

The ASSASSIN *comes out of hiding, and creeps up on the* YOUNG MAN *who has his back turned to him. Strikes him hard with the dagger.*

ASSASSIN: Got you this time, bitch! Die and rot in hell!

The YOUNG MAN *sinks to the floor almost without a sound. The* ASSASSIN *looks around.*

ASSASSIN: Thomas, where are you? Where's the little idiot hiding? Thomas!

YOUNG MAN: (*Weakly*) I'm here.

ASSASSIN: You?! Christ! What were you doing in the Queen's dress?

YOUNG MAN: What? But you... told me... woman's dress...

ASSASSIN: What a mess!

YOUNG MAN: ...and then you go and butcher me! ...Who's the biggest arsehole now?

GROSSLADY: (*Entering*) I be certoso I harked one screaming... Who wouldst thou be? Helpo! A bloke! A priesto assassino!

The ASSASSIN *moves towards* DAME GROSSLADY.

ELIZABETH: (*Offstage*) What is it, Dame Grosslady? Why are you screaming?

GROSSLADY: Dinna budge, Queenie! Shutty the Rory O'More! There be an assassino par here, and he be espying for thee, Queenie!

ASSASSIN: Damn bitch! Shut your trap or I'll kill you!

He threatens DAME GROSSLADY *with the pistol. She runs off behind the bed and immediately re-enters from the left. She goes to her basket and gets out two jars, points them at the* ASSASSIN *as if they were pistols; while she's doing all this, she shouts.*

GROSSLADY: The buzzies! Helpo! The buzzies!

The ASSASSIN *fires at the* DAME. *She avoids the shot, and shakes the jars to get the wasps angry. The* ASSASSIN *starts twitching as if he's been attacked by a swarm of wasps. He drops the pistol and runs off behind the bed jumping and slapping himself like a madman.*

GROSSLADY: Tha axed for this, swine! Duello with buzzies and pops!

ELIZABETH: (*Offstage*) Open the door, Dame Grosslady! That's an order!

GROSSLADY: Dinna entrare, Queenly. The chamber be buzzing with the stabbing buzzies!

The ASSASSIN, *half hidden by the hanging, has opened the backside of the horse and mimes getting into it. He is so preoccupied by trying to do this and not be seen by the two women who are coming in, that he holds on to the hanging to help himself in and inadvertently pulls the whole thing down. We understand that he has hidden himself inside the horse.*

GROSSLADY: Be artful! Draw a snot-rag o'er thy mush!

ELIZABETH *enters, followed by* MARTHA. *She is wearing a veil to cover her face.*

GROSSLADY: Guardies!

She shouts offstage. Two GUARDS *come in. They try to protect themselves from the wasps by slapping themselves all over. Following* DAME GROSSLADY's *command, they run behind the bed looking for the* ASSASSIN.

ELIZABETH: Where has he got to?

GROSSLADY: He was par ici erstwhile… I mind he must needs have ascended the chimbley.

ELIZABETH: Did you say he was disguised as a priest?

GROSSLADY: Nay. He must needs have been a veritable vicar… one of they fly-blown dunsters who hold thee the cross to canoodle wi' one mitt, and wi' t'other mitt they be tugging the string that'll drop thee, and with t'other mitt they be setting the fire undersotto thy trotters and benedicketting thee with t'other mitt… these vicars be possessed of a might of mitts!

ELIZABETH: Do something about these damn animals! Throw the window open!

GROSSLADY: Nay, attend. I have the Queenly buzzie here. T'others need pimply sniff her and they'll wing it dentro the pottle… Coo-ee! Mingle mangle cum buzzies! Your

Queenie callios you! Guarda the buzzies winging it! Upsy
daisy! Damndammit! The Queenie hath buzzed off…
Where hath she fleed? O guarda! She hath winged it dentro
the prancer's nosehole and tutti the buzzies be thripping
after her. That be that then. Finito the perilsome.

*The two women remove the handkerchiefs they had over
their faces, and only now does* ELIZABETH *notice the
wounded* YOUNG MAN *who is lying on the floor.*

ELIZABETH: Thomas! O my God! They have stabbed you
instead of me!

She kneels down and holds him.

YOUNG MAN: (*Speaks with great difficulty*) He mistook me…

ELIZABETH: Yes, yes… I understand… O my sweeting, you
have saved my life!

YOUNG MAN: No… I meant to… I'm sorry!

ELIZABETH: What are you sorry for?

YOUNG MAN: That… dagger… was for… you…

ELIZABETH: O my God! Quick, Martha, get a doctor… so
much blood!

YOUNG MAN: He couldn't even… look me in… the face…
bastard priest… one slash with the knife… and off…! 'Play
the woman…' he tells me… 'With a candle in your arse.'

GROSSLADY: O!

MARTHA: He's rambling, poor little soul… He's going…

GROSSLADY: He be bonkers… hark to him drumbling and
mumping.

YOUNG MAN: 'Open the arse… I'll get in there…' he says…
and then he says… 'No, in the chimney…' And he says to
me… 'Play this pipe!' …I never blew it… but he…
WHACK me… just the same!

GROSSLADY: He parleys mucho filth.

YOUNG MAN: And then he gets into… the horse's belly… like
the Trojan horse… and now the wasps are eating him alive.

(*He laughs*) Ha ha ha.

ELIZABETH: Don't laugh, Thomas. You've got a knife in your belly... It's not good for you... you'll see, you'll pull through...

THOMAS *dies in* ELIZABETH's *arms.*

GROSSLADY: Nay, nay. He be brown breaded. But he brown breaded contento... He was larking...

ELIZABETH: O God, O my God! It was me! It was my fault! (*She leaves* THOMAS *lying on the floor and gets up*) My life is full of corpses. I am a murderess.

She exits upstage.

MARTHA: (*Following* ELIZABETH) That's not true. It was just chance. An accident!

GROSSLADY: Si, a chanceo accidento! Guarda the brazen fortuna of these queenbees! They clapperclaw young dimberdambers into the four toaster to toast theyselves, and the dimberdambers – young groutheads – facket them the favore to take a stab in the stern as a thank you tip. And they facket theyselves to be cozied and mozied, tongued and grovelled... But mio... If I dicket to some young dimberdamber, 'Gimme a smacker,' he respondies me... 'Hike off, trollop!'

EGERTON *enters, followed by the* GUARDS.

EGERTON: If I may... what has happened... ?

GROSSLADY: There hath been a vitriolic vicar and he hath stabbed and morted her.

ELIZABETH *and* MARTHA *re-enter.*

EGERTON: Was she one of your waiting maids?

ELIZABETH: Yes... a male maid... I dressed him up for a bit of a laugh.

MARTHA: (*Under her breath*) Don't talk nonsense. (*To* EGERTON) It's shock, you see. (*To* ELIZABETH, *in a low voice*) For pity's sake, there are guards here too! (*Pointing to the corpse*) Take her away...

The GUARDS *carry* THOMAS *out;* EGERTON *follows them.*

ELIZABETH: It's just rubbish. It's no use any more.

GROSSLADY: Guarda! The prancer hath the wibble wobbles!

MARTHA: So it has... And it seems to be neighing!

The groans of the ASSASSIN *inside, who is being eaten by the wasps, sound like neighing.*

GROSSLADY: Sembra he be throwing a frenzy fit! Tutti the buzzies dentro must be thumping a great battaglio.

ELIZABETH: That's enough! I'm going mad! I'm having nightmares again! Who is responsible for this sorcery? (*Threatening*) It is you, Dame Grosslady... You are a sorceress! It was you! You must be part of this plot... They sent you here... (*Shouts offstage*) Egerton! Guards! (*To* DAME GROSSLADY) Who sent you? Speak! (DAME GROSSLADY *is paralysed with terror*) I'll have you hung up by your feet from a butcher's hook until you confess!

GROSSLADY: Nay, nay tortura, nay!

ELIZABETH: Guards! Egerton! Seize her!

EGERTON *and the* GUARDS *run on and seize the* DAME.

GROSSLADY: Nay, Your Majestical... Pardonare me.

MARTHA: That's enough, Elizabeth! This woman saved your life just now... and look how you're treating her!

ELIZABETH: Let go of her... I'm sorry, Dame Grosslady... forgive me... I allowed myself to be carried away with fear.

GROSSLADY: Nay, Your Ladleship, dinna fash thyssen. It be comprehensive. It be normalo. When a Queenie doth take a frit, what can she confectionate to render hersen tranquillo? She pimply strings up a servitude by the trotters, and opla! Least said soonest blended. It be perfetto naturalo... Now I hath e'en besquittered my pettitose naturalo...

Lifting her skirt so she can go faster, she runs off.

ELIZABETH: (*Who has regained control of herself*) Egerton, a few hours ago, I asked you a question: why has there still been no sign of the delegation of Lords going to Essex House?

EGERTON: A great misfortune, Your Majesty...

ELIZABETH: What misfortune?

EGERTON: Essex and his followers have not kept their promises. No sooner had the Lords entered Essex House, than they were set upon and locked up.

ELIZABETH: But Essex has gone totally demented... I send the Lords to him so they can come to an agreement, and he locks them up?

EGERTON: That is, unfortunately, what took place.

ELIZABETH: When did this happen?

EGERTON: Late last night.

ELIZABETH: Last night? Just a moment... a few hours ago you told me that the meeting had been postponed.

EGERTON: I did not wish to distress you, ma'am. I was hoping to be able to put everything to rights today.

ELIZABETH: (*Ironic*) Your concern for me... is very touching, Egerton! (*Serious*) Were there any fatalities at the time of this offensive?

EGERTON: Yes, the entire escort... all of them cut to pieces.

ELIZABETH: All of them? And the Lords?

EGERTON: Safe.

ELIZABETH: Are you sure?

EGERTON: As soon as all four of them signed the letters...

ELIZABETH: (*Amazed*) What letters?

DAME GROSSLADY *returns.*

EGERTON: The letters written in the Lords' own handwriting in which they plead for the release of the twenty-four prisoners in exchange for their own freedom.

ELIZABETH: Twenty-four prisoners? I knew nothing about this!!

EGERTON: Your Majesty, they are those prisoners we took yesterday afternoon following the skirmish.

ELIZABETH: What skirmish??!!! Keep calm. Let me go over this again. So: I order you to send the Lords to Robert of Essex. Then, a few hours later, there is a skirmish, in the course of which twenty-four of the plotters are captured. Then the Lords go to Essex House, and he, justifiably furious because you have broken the truce, slaughters the entire escort and imprisons the Lords. Is that correct?

EGERTON: Yes. That is correct.

ELIZABETH: And why were there four of them? I ordered you to send two.

EGERTON: Secretary Cecil thought it would be better, he thought it would lend more prestige to the delegation to send the Earl of Worcester and the Lord Keeper of the Seal as well.

GROSSLADY: We facket tuttithing great and grandissimo here!

ELIZABETH: Splendid! You propose, you dispose... all without consulting me. You make me out to be a hallucinating halfwit... It was only a nightmare... The screams. The shots. Everyone in cahoots, starting with my Lady of the Chamber. And you too, Dame Grosslady.

Moment of embarrassment for DAME GROSSLADY, *who was attempting to disappear out of the left door.*

GROSSLADY: Ah, it be vino veritas, Your Ladleship... I harkened the shistol pots, but he dicket me... Sir Thomas, willst tha no helpo me out of this trappola?

EGERTON: Yes, Your Majesty, it was I who ordered them to keep silent. In order to avoid distressing you. We certainly never imagined things would turn round like this...

GROSSLADY: Desideri me to callo the gardies? I will preparare the hook for thee to string him up by his trotters.

She laughs.

ELIZABETH: You never imagined? Who are you trying to fool? You, Bacon, and Secretary Cecil imagined nothing else! It's crystal clear! You organised the trap yourselves to get rid of Robert of Essex.

DAME GROSSLADY *has got a wooden stick and a metre of material out of her basket. She begins to measure* EGERTON *for a coffin.*

GROSSLADY: O che crafty rapscallion!

EGERTON: (*Aggressively to* DAME GROSSLADY) Will you stop meddling? Will you be silent?!

ELIZABETH: No, she speaks! You're always giving lectures about listening to the voice of the people, and as soon as the people opens its mouth, it's 'Silence!' Well actually, no. She speaks!

GROSSLADY: I parley, I measurey, I bury!

ELIZABETH: Of course, you want to go on proposing and disposing undisturbed. Why don't you put my crown on too...? Why don't you give me a good kick in the arse while you're about it?

MARTHA: Elizabeth, I'm sorry but...

ELIZABETH: And you can shut your mouth, trollop. You're an intriguer just like them... Go away!

MARTHA: No! How dare you treat me like this... I am not one of your Councillors, and I'm not one of your scullery maids either. Do you understand? Because I would like to remind you, in case you'd forgotten, how when that damned sister of yours threw you in the Tower, and all those featherbrained misses and court toadies dropped you like a hot brick – quicker than if you had the pox – I was the only one – daft cow that I am – (DAME GROSSLADY *comes and stands close behind* MARTHA) who went in there with you and kept your spirits up among the rats scrabbling around and the bats hanging on the walls!

ELIZABETH: Yes, I'm sorry...

MARTHA: No. No 'sorries'. You know where you can put your 'sorry'. Stuff it!

GROSSLADY: Ooops, the mopsqueezer be getting serioso...

MARTHA: Now you're going to listen to me... And as what I have to say isn't very pretty, ask your Chief of Police to step outside for a moment.

ELIZABETH: Your pardon, Egerton... We will call you back later...

GROSSLADY: Si, we can calliamo thee later for thy fitting...

EGERTON: Of course, Your Majesty... With your permission...

He exits.

MARTHA: Now then, first of all...

GROSSLADY: Attend till the questman intelligencer be departed. Ecco. Now parley.

MARTHA: Look at the state you're in: head over heels in love... desperate to look beautiful... heart going pitter patter at the very thought of meeting him... You are out of your mind, raving mad, fit for the nuthouse!

GROSSLADY: Martha, I mind thee hadst less perilsome to go tweak the hairs from a lion's cobblers... !

MARTHA: And you can shut your mouth as well! Piss off!

ELIZABETH: No, Dame Grosslady stays! All right, all right, I'm raving mad. I'm ready to be locked up... But you are responsible too, Martha. Who persuaded me to let myself be titivated at the hands of Dame Grosslady... ? The wasps on the breasts, the bloody worms in the ear even?

MARTHA: Yes, because you made me feel sorry for you... There you were, reduced to a snivelling heap. I put myself in your place, and I said to myself: I would do it too. But that's what's so bloody stupid. I'm not the Queen, am I?

ELIZABETH: Yes, and I'm not a human being, am I!? I'm not allowed to have feelings, passions... nothing!

MARTHA: O come off it. No one's forcing you to go on with it… You want to lead the life of an ordinary woman? Well then, chuck it in: abdicate! All I know is that last year… if you could have seen yourself – the state you were in…

ELIZABETH: I would have been disgusted with myself… say it!

GROSSLADY: This carissimo amore of thine must needs have turned thee to a foolish grouthead. He doth paint himself forth so brave and bold, he be questionless capabilo of taking a whimsy to squat his bot on thy bonce, Queenie… assuring first to set thereon a round twilted cushion forby not to scratchle his arse on the pikes of thy diadem. (*To* MARTHA) Right?

MARTHA: Yes.

GROSSLADY: Preciso?

MARTHA: Exactly!

GROSSLADY: Soldio!

ELIZABETH: I can break him when and how I choose… if he goes too far.

MARTHA: (*To* DAME GROSSLADY) Did you hear that? If he goes too far!

GROSSLADY: Ah, amore, amore, it doth even drunk the Allblighty and set his halo tooralooring around his bonce! So. Thus: accordion to thee, he hath not gone o'er the top? He hath set on a revoluzione, he doth confectionate a sham-charade, making feint to come by thy palazzo to tip thee his respectuosos, he doth facket prisonerios of thy yes-mans, he hath massacreed the escorto…

MARTHA: And to cap it all he calls you 'Old hunchback'!

GROSSLADY: 'Old Crunchback'! Unpardonabilio. Let a ruffian call thee duncipated, let him call thee a bracket-faced slamkin, let him call thee 'stinking trollop'… 'Trollop'… I pardono thee, I amore thee for that… but let him call thee 'old'… Chop him to messes! Whack! Whack! Whack! Short arse thus! I should coco…

ELIZABETH: Yes, he shouldn't have called me that... that was naughty...

MARTHA: Elizabeth, stop this. It's high time you gave up all this cuddling and canoodling, the simpering and sweet nothings!

ELIZABETH: Why? Don't I have the right to make a fool of myself occasionally? To be empty-headed and giddy? Don't I have the right to titivate myself and wallow in the pains of love like every other woman in the world? Don't I!

MARTHA: No you don't! You are the ruler of this country and a woman just by accident.

A moment's silence. Then a complete change of tone.

ELIZABETH: All right then... thank you for the lecture. Be brave. Have Egerton come in. You see, Dame Grosslady, playtime is over. Look at the life I lead: until a few hours ago I was happy, I was getting myself ready for a night of love. (*She is moved*) I was waiting for my Robert to come. But instead, I'm getting ready for a trial whose outcome is a predetermined sentence of death!

GROSSLADY: (*Weeping*) That be forwhy I semper dicket I would ne'er be Queen! Never!

EGERTON enters.

ELIZABETH: Egerton, I ask you to forgive me for forcing you to witness one of my rather pitiful exhibitions just now.

EGERTON: But Your Majesty, what do you mean... ?

ELIZABETH: Allow me to continue. It will not occur again. First of all, please convey my congratulations to Cecil and Francis Bacon... They did well! It was an excellent idea to send the four Lords in order that they should be taken prisoner... And more excellent yet the provocation in the first place of the capture of the twenty-four conspirators, thus forcing Essex and his followers into retaliation. It was a truly exquisite notion. I wish I had thought of it myself. Well done!

EGERTON: Thank you, Your Majesty! I will convey them. It will give them the greatest pleasure, I feel sure.

ELIZABETH: You said that the Earl of Essex had persuaded the four Councillors to write some letters?

EGERTON: Yes, Your Majesty, I have copies of them here... These damn ruffians managed to get them read out in a dozen churches this morning, during the sermon... even in St Paul's Cathedral... If you would care to have a look at them...

He holds the letters out to her.

ELIZABETH: No no... I can already imagine what is written in them... The Lords say they are outraged by our trap... they declare that they too have been the victims of a plot.

EGERTON: Exactly.

DAME GROSSLADY *goes up to* EGERTON *and reads the letter silently.*

ELIZABETH: And then they themselves propose an exchange with the prisoners we are holding... they advise us that as they are faithful servants of the state, it is the duty of the state to save them.

EGERTON: This is amazing! One might say you had dictated these letters yourself.

ELIZABETH: And then they add: 'We are obliged to admit that there have been errors in the government of the country... and that if the conspirators have turned to rebellion, it must be because grave wrongs have forced them to it!'

EGERTON: Yes yes! That's it! Perfect!

GROSSLADY: Dicky bird for dicky bird!

ELIZABETH: What else did they write?

EGERTON: All four of them warn us that in the event of our deciding to sacrifice them... (*He reads*) 'That would be a sign of weakness and not strength on the part of the government and the state.'

GROSSLADY: O I hath harked that elsewhere... I chance not to mind me where… But I harked it…

EGERTON: (*Still reading*) 'And that their deaths would fall on the shoulders of the Queen and the whole of England.'

GROSSLADY: A diverso versione…

EGERTON: And they end with a threat. (*As before*) …'Our deaths would signal the start of disaffection with your government and your credibility…'

GROSSLADY: Tutto copiato!

ELIZABETH: What arrogance.

MARTHA: You have to do something fast, Elizabeth.

ELIZABETH: Did you say that these bastards have made copies of these letters and that they're distributing them all round the city?

EGERTON: Yes. Someone, whom we have already identified, has even managed to print them… and they're being sold like ballad sheets.

ELIZABETH: What an excellent sense of propaganda!

EGERTON: I have already given the order for them to be seized and the printing presses to be closed down… and to prevent them from selling any more.

ELIZABETH: That's a mistake! That will simply arouse curiosity and they'll start going like hot cakes.

EGERTON: I hadn't thought of that… Very well, I will countermand the order immediately.

ELIZABETH: Organise sermons all over the city. Print your own pamphlets and distribute them…

EGERTON: It will be done…

Begins to leave.

ELIZABETH: Just a moment… What are you going to write in these pamphlets? It must be done with care… You must consult Bacon. Rule One, in war as in peace, if they take one of your men prisoner and demand a ransome, you must bring down the price of the goods that the enemy is holding... so devalue... devalue.

GROSSLADY: God, what a brainbox she hath! She sembras a bloke!

EGERTON: That will be difficult... The Lord Chief Justice and the Lord Keeper of the Seal are highly thought of by the people...

ELIZABETH: We will say that they are great statesmen, but now, poor souls, they are not to be trusted... Perhaps they have been tortured, or even drugged... They are no longer capable of rational thought... They are lost to us... perhaps they have been driven insane.

GROSSLADY: I hath harked that also, but I mind me not where...

MARTHA: Well done, Elizabeth, this is more like your old self...

EGERTON: The trouble is these damn plotters haven't left us much time. They demand a reply before this evening. At sunset they will start throwing the hostages off the walls, one by one.

GROSSLADY: Not frombye the walls! AAAAAUUUUUOOORGH!!!

She mimes someone falling from a great height. The sound of a terrible crash – 'CRRRAAAASH!' – mimes that the person who has fallen has been made very small.

GROSSLADY: Those eternity boxes get tiddlier every minuto!

ELIZABETH: In that case there is no time to lose. Summon the two Chambers immediately. I will go and see them myself. If necessary I will speak in the Cathedral as well. I already have an idea of what I need to say. I will say that I am beside myself... that's logical... in despair... I will lower my voice... I will deliver a moving tribute to the four Councillors... and then I will burst out: 'But we cannot yield! This is the time to hold our ground! We cannot lower ourselves to make compromises with criminals!'

GROSSLADY: It doth smite our heart, it doth slice us to the

nick, but we be obligato to sacrificiare these our dear
brethren... A peck on the mush for the grieving trouble and
strife, a peck for the orphelini dustbin lids, and a boot up
the Khyber for the pooch! AAAARGH!

*She mimes the kisses and the final kick at the dog which shits
itself and runs off.*

ELIZABETH: The state cannot yield!

EGERTON: So we leave them no way out?

ELIZABETH: No!

EGERTON: Like saying to the bastards: go on, kill them... in
fact you'd be doing us a favour...

ELIZABETH: Precisely... with the situation as it stands now...
with everything they've written and distributed... our eyes
are brimming with tears... but...

GROSSLADY: They will haviamo a funeralo di stato!

ELIZABETH: Send for me as soon as the two Chambers have
convened. Farewell, Egerton.

EGERTON: I will fly, Your Majesty... I will return shortly.

He exits.

MARTHA: Well done!

GROSSLADY: Brava! Brava!

ELIZABETH: (*In despair, but controlling herself*) Leave me
be. I am dying. With these other four corpses on his hands,
Essex is well and truly done for now... he's dead already,
and I am dying with him.

MARTHA: No. There may still be time for him to save himself.

ELIZABETH: No, Martha. He won't save himself... Give me
a drink. A strong drink.

MARTHA: No, that's bad for you.

ELIZABETH: Give me my leaves.

MARTHA: No, dearest, you know they give you
hallucinations.

ELIZABETH: The grand finale of the last act is beginning. Just like in *Hamlet*.

GROSSLADY: Back to this obfuscation with Omelette.

ELIZABETH: I am ill. Robert, don't leave your house... they will take you to the Tower... and I will have to seal your death warrant. O Robert... Robert... I am a madwoman... I am hysterical... I can't control myself. Help me. I am swelling up. I am having one of those attacks I had three years ago...

GROSSLADY: We must needs puttiamo her trotters dentro this basinetto of acqua.

ELIZABETH: I am swelling up.

GROSSLADY: Go to, we shall unpin thy laces bedietro.

ELIZABETH: My feet are exploding... quick, take my shoes off... and my stockings.

GROSSLADY: The stampers... away with the stampers.

ELIZABETH: Look, my legs are swelling up. My hands are swelling too. Take my rings off.

GROSSLADY: Acqua.

From this point onwards, DAME GROSSLADY's *interventions must be calm and must not disturb* ELIZABETH's *dramatic monologue.*

ELIZABETH: Goddamned rings, they're stuck to my fingers. Here's the smell of the blood still. I tell you yet again, they're buried, they cannot come out of their graves. Their little, little graves somewhere upon the Queen's high hands: here lies my mother; here a pretty dimpled boy I decked in rags of state; here's Leicester; here's a Lord still sweating on an errand for his Queen. Last ring of all that ends this strange eventful litany. Is Mary Stuart. Come, detested kite; not Afric owns a serpent I abhor more than thy fame and beauty. What, was it you that would be England's Queen? Rejoice! Rejoice and let thy severed head besport itself as 'twere a clodpole at a rustic feast. I fear no more the heat of your blood. And yet you were the captive I held hard for eighteen years. Alive! But how you struggled in the stone embrace of fortress walls as ever and anon your eyes turned to the sea, seeking the ships of Spain. They were the enemy without my gates, and you, pale Queen, the enemy within. More deadly than the adder fanged, and so… NOOOOO!!!! Give her another head. Bind up her neck. Have mercy, Jesu!

MARTHA: Wake up Elizabeth… wake up.

ELIZABETH: Soft, I did but dream; I prithee, hold my eyelids up. Suffer me not to sleep… What do I fear? Myself? There's none else by. Elizabeth loves Elizabeth. That is I am I. Is there a murderess here? No. Yes. I am. And I am bound upon a wheel of fire, but from this torment I will free myself, or hew my way out with a bloody axe. Yet why's my body weak and smooth but that my soft condition and my heart should well agree with my external parts?

Gun shots off.

GROSSLADY: Guarda. They be shootering. They have attrapped Roberto of Yes-Sex. He be prisonero.

ELIZABETH: The ships of Spain are here! The multitudinous seas encumbered quite. Sail upon sail, high sided forty cannoned whales of death. And on my side a clutch of pirates, earth's mere scum, enlisted but for drink… Turn my sweet hellhounds, turn and hear me speak! No, not the weighted words my Parliament will wag their beards at. Not the sceptred isles and stiffened sinews, precious jewel set in a silver sea, that never did nor never in the field of human conflict shall lie at the proud foot of a conqueror. Not all that crap. Hear me, you common cry of curs, now hear Elizabeth, you vagabonds and bastards… I am no taper of true virgin wax. I feed on fear like you; taste bile; need blood. My father was the first to name me bastard but so what? I live. I rule; howe're I was begot.

Elizabeth expects each man this day will fight for booty and if you will not, I'll be up your arses with a fiery torch. I need no heroes – clowns who fight for honour. What makes a hero but the happy accident of time and place; a thief

upon the winning side who writes his own deeds in the
shifting sands of history. Strike your foe-men! I need to see
the English Channel foaming with much blood. Now God
stand up for bastards!

Cease your smiling, Mary, for we have in our hands a
piece of paper the which will give us peace in our own time.
Your death warrant. Who bears the palm of this most heavy
deed? Davison... the Keeper of the Seal... convey him to
the Tower. Burleigh, my Councillor? Him too... Now let
them feel how wretched are those men that hang on
monarchs' favours.

It is the only way. The general ear ne'er hearkens to a
trial where Queen eats Queen in dainty banqueting. Mary,
arise and walk. Love is Time's fool, sweet sister. Come, the
bell invites you. Sing on, my choristers, sing on. Give her
excess of it that surfeiting her appetite may sicken and so
die... How fair you look, as pale as monumental alabaster,
yet the brightness of your eye would shame the stars as
daylight doth a lamp. Now bend up all your spirits to their
full height. Tall. Regal. Then down you kneel, down, down,
your hair like glistering Phaeton, tie it back. I pray you sir,
undo that button. So farewell, a long farewell to all your
revels now are ended in a sleep of death. And from this
instant there's nothing serious in mortality, all is but wanton
boys that cut me to the brains. I am Queen Elizabeth still.
And as the poet says:

> When the tiger and the panther kissed,
> The smaller-mouthed soon lost her head I wist.

Look at your audience. Where be their smiles now
Mary? You knot of mouth friends. Blood and a severed
head are your perfection. This is Mary's last, who stuck and
spangled with your flatteries now pays in Lethe spattered in
your eyes.

> Watch. I order you to watch.
> And where the offence is let the great axe fall.
> The hiss.
> Useless imbecile!
> Clumsy butcher!

She lives yet.
Strike again.
Again.
At last...
Cover her head: its eyes accuse: she died slow.
Sound drums and trumpets; farewell sour annoy,
For here I hope begins our lasting joy.

It's a trap.

Here's hell. Here's darkness. Here is the sulphurous pit.
Burning, scalding, stench, consumption.

That isn't Mary's head.
It is my head...
It is my head...
It is my head......

APPENDIX

In the Italian version of Elizabeth, *Dame Grosslady speaks in dialect. Where this translation departs from the original is indicated by a line in the margin, and a literal translation is given below.*

ACT ONE

Page 22

I wear it simply to cover up the ugly countenance that lies beneath it, Your Ladyship.

I hope you won't find it too frightening, Your Majesty. (*Takes mask off*) Well, this is the real me.

It's no use talking in French... as I understand it perfectly, Magnificent Lady. I know that I look like a man, an ogre... and not even very graceful. Don't make me feel more ashamed than I already do... and don't be afraid of me, my sweet queen. I am a good simple creature, and I am here to help you. (*She goes... etc*)

We call this a walker... or a stroller... and we use it to teach you how to walk on whore's clogs without falling off.

Page 23

These, look. (*Shows her two things... etc*) Pattens with soles three feet high.

The whores in Venice wear them to make themselves look taller.

But Milady, those whores earn a fortune!

Queen, if you prefer it, we can leave you the way you are.

Don't upset yourself, Magnificence. (*She slips*) Oooops! What have I slipped on... what's all this wet stuff! I might be wrong, but it seems to be...

Him? A wooden horse that pisses? That's good luck.

O well then...

Come along, get up, Magnificence... Hurry up and get into the stroller... (*They help... etc*) Good, that's the way. Now we'll shut you snug inside... You can help me, Lady Martha.

Page 24

O look at the queen... commanding over all... A miracle of height!

Would you like a dummy to suck, My Lady?

You don't want to compare yourself with that wooden pisser.

Walk, walk my sweet beanpole...

Come along, come along dearie... settle your bum down here on the chair while I prepare the ointment I'm going to smear on you.

Page 25

Ah Hamlet... I know him... I saw it at the Globe... played by that actor... when he came out with that terrible: 'Take yourself off to a nunnery Ophelia... Any husband of yours would be the greatest cuckold in the world! Take yourself off to a convent...' Ha, ha, ha, ha... (*She gets a jar... etc*)

Oh no... my voice is a bit off just now.

Flowers of alum.

It's perfectly normal, my lady.

Page 26

Beautiful... how does it go? 'The frog at the bottom of the well thought that the arse end of the bucket was the sun...' Splendid!

I've got it now! It's like seeing a reflection in a mirror! A reverse image!

See? Biggedy show-off!

Hold your own tongue. Go and put the clogs away. (*To Elizabeth*) Really, I don't know where you get your servants from, Queen.

Page 27

Take off your shift. Get undressed.

What are you ashamed of? We're all women. The only male here is the wooden pissing horse.

Don't be so naughty. You shouldn't put yourself down all the time. You're still a good-looking woman.

He's playing a sort of drag dressing up game in the mirror.

Listen why don't you stop pulling her leg and taking the piss out of her.

Page 28

You see how it balances out? Tit for tat...

What a muddle of families...

The mirror image exactly! Exactly!

Shall I answer? But for the last time, mind you.

Well then. The Queen, Elizabeth of England, everyone knows, has one terrible weakness: when she sees curtains or tapestries moving... she always has a sword to hand... 'A ghost!' she cries... 'Thwack!' ... and whoever's hiding behind it... never mind. (*She mimes... etc*)

Page 29

Really, and she didn't stab you? Queen, you really should put in a bit more practice... You shouldn't have missed a cow like this one... Anyway, Hamlet has this weakness too... there's a scene where a tapestry moves and Polonius is behind it...

Oh what an allegory! Don't you see?! So, here we have this Polonius, who is the allegory for Cecil, and he's behind a curtain, and there's Hamlet talking to his mother, telling her the most terrible things... saying 'How could you marry that terrible man... slag!' That's how he talks to her... And then at a certain point the arras moves... AAARGH! A rat! WHACK!! You know over there in Denmark they have rats five and a half feet tall... five feet nine at the very least... SPLAT! The sword thrust! CLUNK! Polonius, the allegory, flat on the ground... (*To Martha*) And the next allegory is you...

You don't agree with me? All right. I'll give you a second example. At the end of *Hamlet*, who arrives to sort out the shit heap?

Fortinbras of Norway. Good. And in this shitheap we call
England, who, according to the Puritans, is the Fortinbras
who's going to come from the north and sort it all out?

Page 30

James of Scotland, who is perched on the border ready to
come crashing down on your head, Queenie. (*She gives a
violent tug... etc*)

It's just because I'm keen.

Mongol indeed! You look wonderful... Look here, I've
completely got rid of your double chin.

You're right. You had a double nape!

I got it! Shall I explain?

No. I will tell her. The thing is, the actor who plays Hamlet is
called Richard Burbage. I know him well. He's a man of forty
two... on a good day he doesn't look a day over sixty two...
sixty four... He's got a little bit of a pot belly... and
unbelievably short of breath... every time he performs, after
a bit he gets asthma... and during the duel, when he's with
Laertes – Laertes is young, he jumps, he takes great leaps...
Look what Richard Burbage does in the duel... he knits...
(*She mimes knitting*) ... So at a certain point... although he's
not actually moving, he goes 'Arh, arh, arh'. (*Panting sound*)
And the Queen says to him... 'O Hamlet, you're not a boy any
more, you're breathing through your arsehole!' Shakespeare,
eh? Then they censored it... but that's what he wrote... Well
then, this Burbage is covered in sweat...

Page 31

Yes that's true... he walks all crooked, with his feet turned
out. But when he's acting... he has such power, he intoxicates
the whole audience... (*She acts out in nonsense talk... etc*)

And you understand everything he says. He's a force of nature... even if he is a bit camp.

It shows. It shows... all he needs is the feathers growing out of his arse... And why did they give the part to this numbskull? There must be at least five other actors in the company who would have made a better job of it: younger, thinner, better actors... why did they pick this woofta?

Well, you can't say that any more. Not about your face anyway. Feel how firm it is! (*She gets Elizabeth out of the chair... etc*)

Page 32

We've got to get rid of belly, haven't we?

Slugs. (*Shows her... etc*)

No. Leeches suck your blood. These sluggies only suck fat... Oooh... They suck like... Look how lovely they are. And their little blue eyes... perky little thingies...

Yes. And on your hips and thighs too.

On the shoulders, the arms. And on the widow's hump at the back of your neck.

And on your back, and your bottom... They'll slim you beyond belief. Look at the beasties! Look how greedy this one is! Attila! Caligula!

O how vulgar. The F-word from a queen. And in front of these shy little worms as well. Look at this one, he's gone quite pale. Suck away dearie.

Page 33

And now I've got the key to this whole mirror image business of his... So, for example, when he says 'Denmark is a prison'... he means 'England is a prison'...

O yes... at the end there are dead bodies all over the place. Laertes run through over here; the poisoned queen gasping over there... the king vomiting here... and Hamlet breathing his last there...

Hamlet's. Everyone knows it's Hamlet's fault because he can never make up his mind, he dithers around... He could have resolved everything long before: he stabbed his treacherous uncle right there, when he was praying. 'Now I'll stab him... No. Hang on a minute'... he said to himself... 'I'd be doing him a favour, because he'd die purified of all his sins, and he'd go straight to heaven. My father, on the contrary, died full of sin, and Boom!, he went to hell. I'll wait till my uncle goes into the bedroom with my mother and they start doing dirty things together... ' And then he gets out the knife... 'No. I won't do it now... tomorrow... we'll see... the day after tomorrow... I don't know... maybe next week... ' O God, he could have resolved the whole thing in the first scene, when the ghost of Hamlet's father came on, came to him and said: 'Ha-a-amlet...' – The Ghost father had an echo, like all self-respecting ghosts – 'Ha-a-a-amlet, it's your u-u-u-ncle, he's the assass-ass-ass-i-i-in... stab hi-i-im...'

Page 34

I couldn't give a damn about five acts... and then there's Ophelia dying, and that other one who goes off his head... goes to England, comes back... then the duel. Phew! I like things to be clear. Only one act, but clear. The father's ghost comes on and says: 'Hamlet, he's the murderer!' O, is he? Right you are then!' Out with the knife. 'Assassin'... But no, we get: 'Now I come to think of it, I'll wait and see, I'll put it off, I'll hold on...'

Noooo!

O no, silly woman... the slugs are all squashèd. O what a disaster. It's just like the end of *Hamlet*. You've even squashed the queen.

Squashing slugs? They're right.

Page 35

It's because you're too good to them, and you let them go on prattling... if I was you... whack!!

It's not my finger. It's one of the little wormies that's crawled into the hole...

It's not my fault if worms like greasy holes, is it?

I can't hang on to him... O there he is... Ooop-la! ...I've got him! Look how fat he is! What lovely little eyes!

...All these new worms on the floor... Just look... (*Elizabeth goes off, followed by Martha, to get dressed*) Look what a feast this one's had. He's so plump! OOOH, my goodness these slugs have got fat... They're so full of fat it makes you sick... now I'm going to go straight home to my husband, he's a fisherman. And when I give him these fattened worms, he'll go crazy... he'll go straight out fishing... he'll stick these worms on his hooks and throw them right to the bottom of the river. And the minute they see these worms, the fish will appear: 'The slugs!' EOUGH! And tonight we'll have a huge fish to eat. Ha ha ha... Now I come to think of it, we won't be eating a fish, because these worms have eaten the queen, and the fish eat the worms... so really what we'll be eating is the queen! What about that for a clever idea, eh! What about that for an allegory! To tell you the truth, I didn't make up that little parable... it wasn't me who made it up... It was Shakespeare... actually it was his idea. When he makes Hamlet say: 'A king will sit down at a banquet. Not to eat, but to be eaten... because he is dead and the worms will eat his corpse... A fisherman will walk by... and he'll take a handful

of worms from the king... and he will go fishing. He catches a
big fish! And a poor man, the lowest of the low, finds this fish
and eats it. At the end of it all, the beggar eats the king! It's
enough to give you the shivers! What a brain, that
Shakespeare! You can't have a single idea that he hasn't
copied already!

Page 36

O no, it's certainly not your imagination, queen... you must
be thinner. You only have to see how swollen these beasties
are from sucking at you... They look pregnant.

You call that a little miracle! If you give me time I can even
resurrect the breasts for you too... I'll give you two titties so
big that when you try to cross your arms, it'll be like resting
them on a shelf... you'll be able to put a vase of flowers on
them and water them every morning... O how beautiful!
What a dress!

Page 37

Yes, he'll be reeling. Almost as much as I am now with this
story of you being Hamlet's double.

I'm sorry, queen, but I don't agree. Come on now! A
rebellion organised by theatre people? Can you see them, all
the thespians with their wooden swords and their cannons
loaded with talc and face powder? 'Ready for the rebellion!
Load the cannons! Fire!' BOOM BOOOM! (*She mimes the
explosion... etc*) End of the rebellion!

Page 38

(*Under her breath... etc*) She's playing the part of Hamlet.
He's a sort of pansified transvestite, with feathers in his arse,
and he's taking the piss out of the queen...

(*She explains – 'mimes' – the plot... etc*) ...and that's the end of Act One! (*To Elizabeth*) My Lady, I have to explain this to him because he doesn't know anything about Hamlet. He must be a policeman... (*She continues to explain...*) ...end of Act Four!!

Page 39

I've nearly finished Act Five!

You'd see that *Hamlet* is a sort of drag act, making fun of the queen... and he's stuck at the bottom of a well, disguised as a frog, looking up at the arse end of a bucket saying: 'O what a beautiful sun!'

Page 40

And it can piss too!

No, milady, he doesn't understand.

But look at the expression on his face. He doesn't understand. There's no light in his eyes...

I'm not interrupting, but he doesn't understand.

Page 41

That's not surprising!

I am here checking it word for word to make sure you're not making anything up.

He'll really finish us off!

This is terrible! Now I understand his terrible machinations! This Shakespeare is saying to people: 'What are you up to? Why don't you move yourselves? You consent to being treated like slaves, put upon like beasts of burden, just because you're afraid that if you die you'll burn in hell!

...Arseholes! Hell is here, here on earth! Not down below. Don't be afraid, get on with it, rise up! Kick this shitty government to kingdom come!' (*She begins to sing a revolutionary protest song*)

Page 42

Keep calm! Your brain will explode. It's too much to take in all at one go like that! Take it step by step.

(*She mocks... etc*) PLOP! The egg of harmony! With a miniature Jesuit inside!

And then you can burn it... A gust of wind and some wandering sparks...

Page 43

Beautiful! Beautiful line... what a metaphor! ...Shakespeare? Shakespeare, Shakespeare...

But it was Shakespeare's style!

Ha ha, very good! Shakespeare!
But what does this Shakespeare ever write that's his own, eh? What? Thief!

Page 44

Don't you understand, dear queen... these ruffians have the nerve to come here and kill you.

After I've done you the shelf with the vase of flowers for you to water...

Page 45

Ah! Terrible queen!

Page 46

O Jesus... I must be seeing double. I can't believe my eyes.

Down there, at the end of the street... It looks like your beloved, the Earl of Essex... isn't he handsome... with all his men... O isn't he handsome? They're coming in a procession... some men and women are clapping them.

(*Gets another telescope... etc*) ...Have a look, queen, have a look... I'm really afraid we've had it this time...

It's mine. I brought it back from Venice. They sell them on stalls in the Piazza... with every ten wooden gondolas you buy, they give you one free... Military secret!

I'll go to the door with you.

Page 47

Well said queen! Then at the first whiff of cannon fire they'll piss themselves worse than your horse!

(*She has taken a pen... etc*) I'm ready to take notes... I'll do the writing, your Ladyship...

Wait a minute, I've got to write down the address: 'To the Earl of Essex, Essex House...'

My Lady, if the Lords get lost on the way... then the message would get lost... It doesn't take long to write the address.

'To the Earl of Essex, to be put into his own hands... '

(*She repeats... etc*) 'We come... '

'...the Queen... '

(*As before*) '...to understand... French.'

'To understand the cause.' Full stop! Well, that's clear enough!

Page 48

It was the end of the sentence.

Well then, comma!

Semi colon!

Exclamation mark!

But now I'll have to turn this full stop into something else, won't I? Shall I draw a flower over it? A dragon? Saint George on his horse?

Comma.

'...why certain tickles i'faith... '

Tickles...

(*As one... etc*)'Ah! Tickles!' ...I see the irony now... (*She begins to write... etc*) ...Ah. Ah. 'Tickles' Ah. Ah.

Another queen?

The same queen as before! (*She writes*) 'The queen, the same one as before... '

Page 49

Are they supposed to guess?

'A tissue of lies... '

(*As if to say... etc*) Of lies.

Bless you!

Or not to be, that is the question...

'Dressed... '

'Ah! Dressed!'

'Undressed... '

Ah! You shall have more. Ah! More tickles! (*Elizabeth looks... etc*) 'Shall... '

Just as before. More tickles, just as before... (*She has got to the bottom... etc*)

'Just a... just a... '(*Turns the... etc*)

Page 50

There's no room left for justice! (*She goes... etc*)

Yes, I've got that! Fucking cow!

Stepnitalian! It is understood everywhere!

Ah queen, did you see how pale Sir Thomas turned when you told him about the graffiti against him? I bet Cecil and Bacon have got the shits!

I learned to talk smutty by hanging around queens... fucking cow!

I can do it, but I must warn you it might sting a bit.

Page 51

Yes. From these (*She holds up... etc*)

Buzzies.

First of all, Martha, you take this little piece of sandalwood.
That's to make some smoke. I place the open jar, with the
bees inside, on the breast itself… then I let a bit of smoke
inside… and the bee gets cross and FATANG! He stings you!
Then in a little while you'll see how beautifully the breast will
swell up! Plump! Firm! Taut!

(*Referring to… etc*) O you'd need a hornet for her…

Yes, you can do it with cotton but it doesn't produce the same
result, cotton. There's an old proverb that says 'Cotton is
cotton. It isn't satisfying!' And suppose Robert wants to
stroke you. Anyway a bee sting doesn't hurt very much…
because I'll smear a little honey and myrrh on the breast to
lessen the pain.

Well they won't be like balloons, but I can promise you they'll
be beautiful.

Page 52

Good. Just wait while I smear on the honey and myrrh. Help
me. (*Hands Martha… etc*)

Oh… three days… maybe five… it depends how long we leave
the sting in.

No, no. Half an hour is too long. You'd grow a breast like a
water melon – like this!

Sweet queenliness, take a deep breath.

Go on, Martha. Do the smoke round it. (*She puts… etc*)

Wonderful! That's marvellous! It stung her straight away!
Hurrah!

Don't give in, don't give in... Majesty, I'm going to put a little camphor on it. (*We see her... etc*)

Page 53

No, just a little while longer... wait, my sweetie, don't give in... Look, look, it's swelling up already!

O he's lost his sting now. He's dead. Wait till I get another jar ready... with a new bee...

No, the titties have to swell at the same time... So you can keep an eye on them... You don't want one of them to grow and grow, and the other one to stay as flat as a pancake...

That's normal. Bees' stings always have that effect. Pee as much as you like, we'll blame the wooden pissing horse. Now then, let's go with the second one! (*She applies the second... etc*) Is he stinging?

(*To Martha*) Make some smoke... smoke... (*Turns back... etc*) Stinging now?

O you naughty bee! Don't want to sting eh? Well I'll teach you a lesson! (*She shakes... etc*)

Page 54

No no... Here we are, I've got the avenger! (*Gets another jar... etc*)

An Irish hornet.

Don't be afraid, sweet splendiforousness... It has a more delicate puncture than the bee's. Come along now, don't get agitated. (*Without realising... etc*) Hold her, Martha!

Fool, burning the queen's bum. (*She takes... etc*) Sit down here dear... sit in this basin, the water will cool you down.

Page 55

No, this time you sat on the jar of bees... naughty bee! He didn't want to bite you on the breast, but he bit you on the arse! Catholic! Republican!

ACT TWO

Page 59

Here I am, duckie... How splendiforous! Up on your wooden pissing horse, so early in the morning!

New waspies, dearie.

Good. We call those Venus's love bumps dearie. Hold on tight to the horsie, we're going to go backwards. (*She pushes the horse... etc*)

O that's wonderful dearie. It's an erotic game! The men go potty for it! ...Now we'll take all the hairpins out for you.

No, my lady, there was no battle. I was out and about too. I crossed the whole of London looking for wasps and I didn't hear so much as a dog barking. It was so quiet you could have heard the flies buzzing... the flies that were buzzing in London last night!

Page 60

No?!

No!?

Alive? The head was alive? Like Saint John the Decapitated! Well that would be useful, wouldn't it? Because without turning your head, you could look... (*Mimes holding a head... etc*) ...look over here... look over there...

O no!

A raspberry from the chopped off head.

Bouncing?

Then what?

Page 61

Goddammit, it was right! Where is the woman's head? O yes! She was holding it. All right. Dammit, I understand what it all means. Now I understand. This dream means that the Earl of Essex has lost his head.

He's lost his head from love... of you.

(*To Martha*) While we're on the subject of good news, why don't you tell her who's on his way!

Robert of Essex has decided to come and pay his respects to you. Happy?

You just be careful you don't go out of your head for real... you know what happens to those sort of people... (*Mimes heads... etc*) Bouncies!!

Yes your ladyship. (*Martha helps... etc*)

Page 62

(*Going to the door*) There's no point in knocking. The Queen can't see anyone because she's all undone and looks like she's been dragged through a hedge backwards! (*She peeps... etc*) Your ladyship, it's the chief of police. The bloodhound.

Let him in, my lady, to see what a mess you're in?

Blindfold the chief of police? That would give him a turn!

That's an idea! Come in, Sir Thomas! (*Pulls his hat... etc*) It's the Queen's order that I have to pull your hat well down over your eyes because... O dammit, what a head... Your Ladyship, his head is so big it won't go into the hat... It's so big that if it fell into a headsman's hands he'd jump for joy... there we are... that's got it. Off you go dearie.

There's plenty more where he came from.

Page 63

Answer her, milord.

Smooth tongued bastard! (*Pushes horse... etc*)

Conspirators. Shakespeare is a rebel? Well that's a turn up for the book!

Page 64

(*Gobsmacked*) No! My Lady! Theatricals taking to politics! Unheard of! Whatever next!

She's gone. (*She lifts... etc*) I'll lift your hat. Get a breath of air.

You were lucky you didn't see the look that came into her eyes... wicked, terrifying... just like her sister, Bloody Mary, when she set up the courts of inquisition... There's nothing to be done about it... She's a redhead... she too, just like her father, Henry the Redhead... terrible. A whole family of redheads. All wicked!

There's a proverb in my country that goes: 'Red head at night, Henry's delight. Red head in the morn, prepare to be shorn.'

Page 65

THWACK! The poet's head in the basket too! Do you know,

Sir Thomas, why English coffins are shorter than those anywhere else?

Because in England nearly everyone is buried holding their head in their hands.

(*Swiftly pushing... etc*) Don't laugh so loudly, here's the queen. (*To the queen*) How are you feeling? Better?

It's the voice of your Captain of the Guard.

Page 66

(*Blocking... etc*) Stop! There's a chasm there! It isn't time for the short coffin yet. (*She accompanies Egerton to the door*) Your Ladyship, it is true what the proverb says: 'When justice is blind, the police force is at least squinty and cross-eyed!' ...Let the guards come in, your Ladyshipness, there is great danger.

Don't pass remarks! Busybody, you have no idea what's happened. An extraordinary miracle! Very early this morning, when it was almost still night, well in fact it was still night, before morning... Elizabeth heard a goldfinch crying CHEEP CHEEP in the garden. She went down. And there was the little birdie... CHEEP CHEEP... all frozen cold. She picked him up, the poor little frozen birdie, CHEEP CHEEP, and she put him between her breasts. And she, good Samaritan that she is, came back here to bed, and she put him between the sheets and she blew a little warm air on him, and WHOOSH! CHEEP CHEEP! WHOOSH! This young man sprang out. Straightaway the Queen got down on her knees: 'Saint Rosalie, the most beautiful saint of all, what should I do with this young man?' And the saint answered her: 'CHEEP CHEEP, unite the young man with his little bird!' And that's how it went!

Page 67

Well done! That way he'll be mistaken for an assassin...
CHEEP CHEEP! He'll turn back into a little bird!

Yes, well done. Dress him up as a woman, that's a good idea.

Yes.

Page 68

You are too much. Just mind your head! Bounce!

The try-out boy. The titty tester!

(*Alarmed*) Your Majesty, there is a man... down there in the
garden... in the maze... the guards... are chasing him with the
dogs.

Page 69

It must be that bastard who was trying to climb up into this
room to kill the Queen. Now he's gone over there.

Alive! So that afterwards we can dress him up as a woman as
well. Ha ha!

Let's go! God what fun! It's just one long party here at court.
A coup de theatre every minute. From the window you can
watch a fugitive being chased by dogs. A half naked young
man inside the bed... Just like being at a play!

Page 71

I'd like to know how that man managed to kill himself.

Page 72

Get up! Get up!

Get up on these platform clogs!

O Goddammit! The candlestick's fallen into the fireplace!

Oh, what a lot of smoke! (*We can hear... etc*) Queen, I can hear screams coming from the chimney. Listen to the screams! AAAAAARGH!

Page 73

(*Imitating... etc*)AAAAAAARGH! It's the chimney. It's the voice of the chimney.

It must be the wind!

Do they torture the wind in England too?

That great slag! O no thank you, dearie.

Page 74

(*She has discovered... etc*) O look! A pipe!

The Magic Flute! You can play it even if you don't blow in it! All you have to do is move your fingers!

Give me a kiss in exchange!

Me, old hag? You called me an old hag? I hope lightning strikes you: CCRRRACHK! (*She mimes... etc*) As short as that, clogs and all. (*She goes off...*) A short dwarf!

Page 75

(*Entering*) I'm sure I heard someone screaming. Who are you... ? Help! A man! A killer priest!

Don't move, Queen! Close the door, because there's an assassin in here and he's looking for you!

The wasps! Help! The wasps!

You asked for it, you swine! Duel with wasps and pistols!

Page 76

Don't come in here, Queen, the room is full of the stinging wasps!

Be careful... cover your face with a handkerchief.

Guards (*Shouts off*)

He was here just now... I think he must have got up the chimney.

No. He must have been a real priest, one of those madmen who give you the cross to kiss with one hand while they're holding the rope that's going to hang you in the other hand; and with the other hand they're lighting the fire under your feet, and blessing you with the other hand... These priests have got so many hands!

No, wait. I've got the queen wasp here. The others only have to get a sniff of her, and they'll all fly into the jar... Coo-ee, come on waspies, your Queen's calling you! Look at them coming! They're falling in! Dammit! The Queen's flown out... where is she? O look... she's got into the horse's nostril and all the wasps are following her. That's it then. Danger over.

Page 77

Oh!

He's beside himself... Listen to the way he's talking...

Everything he says has a dirty double meaning.

Page 78

He didn't. He's dead. But he died happy... he was laughing!

Yes, a chance accident! Look what brazen luck these queens have. They haul young lads into bed to warm themselves up, and then these fools do them the favour of taking a blade between the shoulders as a tip as well! And they get themselves cuddled and stroked, licked and nuzzled... But me... If I say to a young man: 'Give me a kiss,' he says to me, 'Shut your face, tart!'

There was a killer priest in here and he stabbed her and killed her.

Page 79

Look, the horse looks as though he's got the shakes.

It looks as though he's having a fit. All the wasps inside him must be having a fight.

No, not torture, no!

No, Your Majesty, forgive me.

No, no milady, don't worry about it. It's understandable, it's normal: when a queen gets a fright, what does she do to relieve her mind? All she has to do is hang a servant on a hook and everything's fine again. That's only natural. I just shat myself of course...

Page 81

We do things on the grand scale.

Yes it's true... I heard the shots... But he told me... Sir Thomas, won't you help me out of this trap?

Your Ladyship, shall I call the guards? I'll get the hook ready so you can hang him up by his feet a bit. (*She laughs*)

Page 82

O what a fine cunning fellow.

I speak, I measure, and I bury.

Page 83

Ooops, the woman's getting heavy...

Yes we'll call you back later and we'll measure you properly.

Wait till the spymaster's gone. There. Now you can speak.

Martha I'd say you'd be in less danger if you went and tried to pull the hairs out of a lion's bollocks.

Page 84

This dear love of yours, his 'Lordship, must surely have turned you into a mental deficient; he's got so above himself he's capable of taking a fancy to sitting on your head, Queenie, making sure to put a cushion on it first so's not to scratch his arse on the spikes of your crown. (*To* MARTHA) Right?

Precisely?

Sold!

Ah, love that inebriates even God and sends his halo whirling round his head! So according to you, he hasn't gone too far yet? He's started a rebellion; he makes a charade of coming to pay homage to you; he takes your councillors prisoner; he slaughters the escort...

'Old hunchback'! That's unforgiveable. Let a man call you a fool, a gibbering idiot, let him call you 'Whore'... 'Whore'! – 'I forgive you, I love you for that.' But if he calls you old...

Chop him down! Whack, whack, whack... down to that.
Come off it dearie...

Page 85

(*Weeping*) That's why I always said I'd never be Queen!
Never!

Page 86

Word for word!

Oh I've heard that somewhere before... I can't remember
where... but I've heard it...

Page 87

...a slightly different version...

All copied!

Page 88

God, what a brain she's got. She's like a man!

I've heard that too, but I can't remember where...

Not off the walls! AAAAUUUUOOORGH! (*She mimes
etc.*) The coffins get shorter all the time!

It breaks our heart, it cuts us to the quick, but we are obliged
to sacrifice these dear brothers of ours! A kiss for the widow,
a kiss for the orphans and a kick for the dog! AAAAARGH!
(*She mimes etc.*)

Page 89

They'll have state funerals!

Brava! Brava!

Page 90

Back to the obsession with Hamlet.

We'll put her feet in this basin of boiling water.

Come on, we'll unlace you at the back.

The shoes, off with the shoes.

Water.

Page 91

Look, they're shooting. They've taken Robert of Essex prisoner!

Methuen's Modern Plays

Bertolt Brecht	*Mother Courage and Her Children*
	The Caucasian Chalk Circle
	The Good Person of Szechwan
	The Life of Galileo
	The Threepenny Opera
	Saint Joan of the Stockyards
	The Resistible Rise of Arturo Ui
	The Mother
	Mr Puntila and His Man Matti
	The Measures Taken and other Lebrstücke
	The Days of the Commune
	The Messingkauf Dialogues
	Man Equals Man and *The Elephant Calf*
	The Rise and Fall of the City of Mahagonny and *The Seven Deadly Sins*
	Baal
	A Respectable Wedding and other one-act plays
	Drums in the Night
	In the Jungle of Cities
	Fear and Misery of the Third Reich and *Señora Carrar's Rifles*
	Schweyk in the Second World War and *The Visions of Simone Machard*
Brecht ⎫ Weill ⎬ Lane ⎭	*Happy End*
Howard Brenton	*The Churchill Play*
	Weapons of Happiness
	Epsom Downs
	The Romans in Britain
	Plays for the Poor Theatre
	Magnificence
	Revenge
	Hitler Dances
	Bloody Poetry

Barrie Keeffe	*Gimme Shelter* (*Gem, Gotcha, Getaway*)
	Barbarians (*Killing Time, Abide With Me, In the City*)
	A Mad World, My Masters
Arthur Kopit	*Indians*
	Wings
Larry Kramer	*The Normal Heart*
John McGrath	*The Cheviot, the Stag and the Black, Black Oil*
David Mamet	*Glengarry Glen Ross*
	American Buffalo
David Mercer	*After Haggerty*
	Cousin Vladimir and *Shooting the Chandelier*
	Duck Song
	The Monster of Karlovy Vary and *Then and Now*
	No Limits To Love
Arthur Miller	*The American Clock*
	The Archbishop's Ceiling
	Two-Way Mirror
	Danger: Memory!
Percy Mtwa Mbongeni Ngema Barney Simon	*Woza Albert!*
Peter Nichols	*Passion Play*
	Poppy
Joe Orton	*Loot*
	What the Butler Saw
	Funeral Games and *The Good and Faithful Servant*
	Entertaining Mr Sloane
	Up Against It
Louise Page	*Golden Girls*
Harold Pinter	*The Birthday Party*
	The Room and *The Dumb Waiter*
	The Caretaker
	A Slight Ache and other plays
	The Collection and *The Lover*

	The Homecoming
	Tea Party and other plays
	Landscape and *Silence*
	Old Times
	No Man's Land
	Betrayal
	The Hothouse
	Other Places (A Kind of Alaska, Victoria Station, Family Voices)
Luigi Pirandello	*Henry IV*
	Six Characters in Search of an Author
Sephen Poliakoff	*Coming in to Land*
	Hitting Town and *City Sugar*
	Breaking the Silence
David Rudkin	*The Saxon Shore*
	The Sons of Light
	The Triumph of Death
Jean-Paul Sartre	*Crime Passionnel*
Wole Soyinka	*Madmen and Specialists*
	The Jero Plays
	Death and the King's Horseman
	A Play of Giants
C. P. Taylor	*And a Nighingale Sang . . .*
	Good
Peter Whelan	*The Accrington Pals*
Nigel Williams	*Line 'Em*
	Class Enemy
Theatre Workshop	*Oh What a Lovely War!*
Various authors	*Best Radio Plays of 1978* (Don Haworth: *Episode on a Thursday Evening;* Tom Mallin: *Halt! Who Goes There?;* Jennifer Phillips: *Daughters of Men;* Fay Weldon: *Polaris;* Jill Hyem: *Remember Me;* Richard Harris: *Is It Something I Said?*)
	Best Radio Plays of 1979 (Shirley Gee: *Typhoid Mary;* Carey Harrison: *I Never Killed My German;* Barrie Keeffe: *Heaven Scent;*

John Kirkmorris: *Coxcombe;* John
Peacock: *Attard in Retirement;* Olwen
Wymark: *The Child*)
Best Radio Plays of 1981 (Peter Barnes:
The Jumping Mimuses of Byzantium;
Don Haworth: *Talk of Love and War;*
Harold Pinter: *Family Voices;* David
Pownall: *Beef;* J P Rooney: *The Dead
Image;* Paul Thain: *The Biggest
Sandcastle in the World*)
Best Radio Plays of 1982 (Rhys
Adrian: *Watching the Plays Together;*
John Arden: *The Old Man Sleeps
Alone;* Harry Barton: *Hoopoe Day;*
Donald Chapman: *Invisible Writing;*
Tom Stoppard: *The Dog It Was
That Died;* William Trevor: *Autumn
Sunshine*)
Best Radio Plays of 1983 (Wally K Daly:
Time Slip; Shirley Gee: *Never in My
Lifetime;* Gerry Jones: *The Angels They
Grow Lonely;* Steve May: *No
Exceptions;* Martyn Read: *Scouting for
Boys*)
Best Radio Plays of 1984 (Stephen
Dunstone: *Who Is Sylvia?;* Don
Haworth: *Daybreak;* Robert Ferguson:
Transfigured Night; Caryl Phillips:
The Wasted Years; Christopher Russell:
Swimmer; Rose Tremain: *Temporary
Shelter*)
Best Radio Plays of 1985 (Rhys
Adrian: *Outpatient;* Barry
Collins: *King Canute;* Martin
Crimp: *The Attempted Acts;*
David Pownall: *Ploughboy
Monday;* James Saunders:
Menocchio; Michael Wall:
Hiroshima: The Movie)